Bob Prophette

The Gospel according to Saint X

No one can teach you what you already know.

THE GOSPEL ACCORDING TO SAINT X

Copyright © 2023 Bob Prophette

All rights reserved.

Imprint: Koan & Co.

Original artworks by Antoine de Saint Exupery from *The Little Prince* book are in the Public Domain. Changes to the originals are the work of the author and can be used with attribution. Wikipedia is the source of the summary of the work which appears in the Appendix. The Summary of the Chapters of *Tolstoy's Gospel's in Brief* are Public Domain. All other rights are reserved.

ISBN: 978-1-7391291-5-6

Introduction

Once, when I was about 54, I read a magnificent book about the world called *The Gospels in Brief*. It contained many strange tales of a man who lived a long time ago in the desert. In the book it said: *God is the spirit in man.* It was written by Leo Tolstoy, this is what he looked like:

The book said that the spirit is invisible to the eye. It reminded me of another book, one that started with a drawing of an elephant inside a snake that only some could see: Antonie de Saint Exupery's *The Little Prince*.

THE GOSPEL ACCORDING TO SAINT X

This is a book I'd missed as a child but came across in adulthood, both because of its widespread love and also because I read it to my daughter. Our copy of *The Little Prince* looked like this:

Many have noted the religious themes in Saint-Exupery's book. It is often referred to as a set of modern parables. People express deep affection for it, but are often unable to recall whether it is a sad book, or a happy one. Quite a few conflate it with Wilde's *The Happy Prince*. Others remember only specific details, like the story of the baobab trees or the vain rose. Some recall the Little Prince as a pilot or the pilot as a little prince.

Or they would mention the various drawings of sheep.

Some, despite remembering a book of that name, failed to recall any of its details.

What surprised me was that none of those who remembered it, seemed to understand it for what it struck me to be essentially about: an assisted suicide. If you don't believe me, read it again and you will see.

It is the story of a mysterious little man, fathered by the universe, who, after becoming enlightened by a wise creature, takes up the offer of an assisted suicide by a demonic animal. He does this as a gift to his friend, so that in the future he will experience joy and live in hope. His friend is a man who has lost his way in life, who needs his innocence and sense of wonder returned to him.

That's how the story looks to me in any case. It's both the story of Adam and the story of Jesus Christ.

Let me explain…

The Prince lives in harmony on his little planet (Eden), until he encounters the vain rose (Knowledge of Good and Evil). He leaves his paradise and encounters characters who personify the worst of human traits (Suffering). He reaches Earth (now as Jesus), hears a secret from a fox (John the Baptist) and is soon presented with the opportunity to redeem himself. He saves the lost soul called the pilot (Mankind), and through this act he finds his way back to paradise, setting us an example of how to live courageously and in freedom.

THE GOSPEL ACCORDING TO SAINT X

When asked, many would consider the book and reply: "But it's only a children's book!"

The book is more than that. Saint-Exupery had a message for the world and *The Little Prince* was how he wrapped it up. It is more engaging than his other attempts, including the long and polemical unfinished manuscript he left to posterity, a book few have read: *The Citadelle* or *Wisdom of the Sands*.

The message is a pretty simple one:

You've lost your way, but don't worry. There is a way back if only you can become a better person.

In Tolstoy's Gospels what has been forgotten is that within each of us is a divine spark. The force that drives the universe. We are born pretty much perfect, but something happens when we grow up that corrupts us. *Like Satan and Adam we fall.* Then, as fallen beings we take our turn in corrupting the next generation. Sometimes we do this in ignorance, sometimes for selfish reasons, but the "means of corruption" are definitely owned by all of us. But then so too are the means of our salvation. We already know the solution. It's within us. As John the Baptist would say: *The Kingdom of God is at hand.*

BOB PROPHETTE

At this point I would like to stress your author is not a Christian. I don't believe in a God. I believe all gods are a work of our imagination and that *The Bible*, as a product of our imagination, is far more important than the God it seeks to describe.

So, if you ever want to judge someone's intelligence, try this experiment: ask them what *The Little Prince* is about.

If what they say doesn't seem to recognise the book as an important philosophical text, a modern Socratic dialogue, then they are probably just 'grown-ups.' You might want to change the topic and talk golf, politics and neckties instead. They'll think you are a very sensible person.

I'm not sure Saint-Exupery read Tolstoy's Gospels. I like to think he probably did. He was brought up as a catholic and is reported to have said he would have liked to be, if not an author, then a priest, or a monk. Perhaps a flying one.

Had he read Tolstoy's Gospels I think he would have approved. I think he would have appreciated the attempt to strip back the four confused and contradictory texts to their enduring, if elusive, essentials. Ironically, Tolstoy achieved this by stripping out from the Gospels anything remotely magical, focusing instead on just what is believed to have been said by Jesus, to the various characters he encounters on his journey. Exupery achieved something similar by putting in as many magical ideas as he could. For example, house sized planets, volcanos you can cook your breakfast on, talking flowers and animals etc. So much so that what he produced is easily thought of as a children's book, and is loved by children.

After *The Bible*, *The Little Prince* is the most widely translated book in history. Like *The Bible* it may have become as widely misunderstood. Both books are symbolised by Saint-Exupery's Drawing No.1 and Drawing No.2. An elephant inside a boa constrictor from the outside and the inside. Presented with Drawing No.1, that of the boa constrictor from the outside, it takes a special quality to see the elephant, enormous as it is.

Learning to see the elephant requires a change of perspective. Tolstoy showed us how to look at *The Bible* differently, it was his apocalypse – his revelation. Through careful study of the original Greek, he was able to show exactly how and why the original story of Jesus, as reported by those who were close to him, had been corrupted to serve the interests of the nascent Church. In very much the same way that Jesus revealed the absurdities and contradictions of orthodoxy, as espoused by the leaders of the Jewish religion in his time. Power corrupts and power protects itself.

Once you know what you are looking for, when you can look at the Gospels anew, it's hard not to see the corruption. Jesus quite clearly had issues with Judaism as practiced in his day. He urged people to think with their hearts. He did not tell them what to do, he showed them and made them question what they had been told.

He was very clear that Heaven isn't a place, and that God isn't something external to man. He was clear that nothing that happens to you makes you 'unclean'. He said we are slaves of comfort, and the rich would never find peace. He said these things in allegorical/metaphorical terms. The fact that they have been confused is like finding that someone believes the Little Prince's planet really is out there…in the vicinity of Asteroid B613.

As a homage to Tolstoy's Gospels and to *The Little Prince*, I decided to try to retell the gospels using the characters from Saint-Exupery's work. I have kept faithfully to the chronology of the story that Tolstoy proposed, as he was faithful, as far as he could be, to the original. My hope is that this retelling will help people better understand both works.

One of the pleasures of reading *The Little Prince* is Saint-Exupery's fine watercolours. Having myself never been encouraged to pursue a career as an artist, I can't hope to impress the readers with my own illustrations, and I hope you will forgive me for using and manipulating the originals, now out of copyright.

I'll start with an image of the little man himself. My Drawing No. 1.

Now if you look at the picture and say to yourself "hey, it's just a picture of the Little Prince with a Jesus face put on it", then maybe this book isn't for you.

In 2020, Julian Baggini wrote *The Godless Gospel*, which is a modern attempt to do what Tolstoy had done. Baggini's analysis of the moral content of Jesus's teaching is very lucid and clear. In particular, the idea that what is needed is not rules and dogma but *Metanoia* – a transformative change of heart. It strikes me that this concept is the same one that the fox reveals to the Little Prince:

It is only with the heart that one can see rightly: what is essential is invisible to the eye.

Saint Exupery's *The Little Prince* is certainly capable of bringing about this Metanoia. This is how Michael Morpurgo described the experience in the forward to his recent translation of the book.

Great books can change us. Having immersed myself so completely in this story, I am sure I will never be able to look up at the stars again without thinking of the Little Prince up there somewhere. And I will look at a flower differently, at people differently...I will think of myself differently too, and try even harder to look after and cherish the child in me. For the child in each of us is the heart and soul in each of us.

THE GOSPEL ACCORDING TO SAINT X

Baggini ended his work with the thought that perhaps it was time for Jesus to die for us again. I don't know about you but I think he's done his bit. Here, I offer the Little Prince to take his place.

BOB PROPHETTE

The Cast

I HAVE ATTEMPTED TO ASSIGN the characters from Saint-Exupery's tale to the Gospels as best I can. Recognising that there are fewer of them and so some, inevitably must play more than one role.

Jesus	The Little Prince
Sin/Satan/Knowledge of Good and Evil	The Rose/Baobab/Echo
John the Baptist	The Fox
The Disciples	The Pilot
Caiaphas	Chief Lamplighter
Pilate	The King
Soldiers/Rome	The Hunters
Various	The Lazy Man The Conceited Man The Tippler The Businessman The Geographer The Switchman

THE GOSPEL ACCORDING TO SAINT X

Oh, and I've added an astronaut for good measure. You'll meet him in Chapter 12.

I don't feel qualified to add to the mountain of interpretation the Gospels have engendered. However, as I have made some changes to the terminology used by Tolstoy I should offer some explanation. To avoid this turning into a polemic, interested readers can consult the Appendix. A synopsis of *The Little Prince* and Tolstoy's summary of the chapters in his *Gospels in Brief* are included for ease of reference.

Chapter One

TOLSTOY'S GOSPELS IN BRIEF begin with a story about Jesus as a child, a story that I think would have suited the Little Prince very much indeed.

*****

The Little Prince, who volunteered very little about himself, and rarely answered questions, said little of his parents. What he did say was no less intriguing than the rest of his tale.

His mother, who lived on another planet at the time, got herself engaged to a man. She had become pregnant before they met, while still a 'virgin'. The kindly man agreed to look after her and raise the child as if it were his own.

And the Little Prince grew and matured and was intelligent, if a little precocious, beyond his years.

Once, the Little Prince's parents took him on holiday, to a planet full of strange sights, statues and temples. At the end of the holiday, the Little Prince's parents set off for home. In their somewhat hectic departure they had forgotten something: the Little Prince. When they stopped to look for him, he was nowhere to be found. They began to be worried. For three days they searched, patiently re-tracing their steps. Imagine their surprise then, when they found him in one of the temples. He was sitting with the teachers listening attentively and asking many questions. He did not look lost at all.

"What are you doing here?" his parents said, more than a little annoyed but very relieved.

The Little Prince told them that he had heard some people call this place the "House of the Father". And so, not having a real father of his own, this is where he came in order to be found.

"What a strange little man you are!" his father said, now much less annoyed.

The Little Prince continued to grow and ask questions, such was his appetite to understand all that went on in the big wide world.

One day the Little Prince heard of a planet where there was a very strange creature that looked something like a fox. He lived in the open and only ate tree bark and flowers. He dressed oddly, seemingly unconcerned with comfort or what others thought.

The fox told people that they would learn to be at peace if only they would love one another and be kind. He said that everything they needed to live at peace in the world was right here. *The Kingdom of God was at hand.* If they could live better lives, they could create a heaven right where they were. But they had to change.

When people asked the fox: "What should we do?" He replied: "If you have two chickens give one of them to someone that doesn't have one."

When another asked him, he said: "Do not take from anyone anything you do not need."

THE GOSPEL ACCORDING TO SAINT X

And to another he said: "Do not hurt anyone or lie to them."

And to yet another: "Appreciate what you have already. You are responsible for what you love."

And to another: "You can only see clearly with the heart. What is important is invisible to the eye."

Many people came to him and despite his strange appearance and behaviour they listened, changed their lives and became more at peace.

Hearing about this strange creature the Little Prince took advantage of a group of migrating birds and paid the fox a visit.

He listened carefully to what the fox said.

Chapter Two

AFTER VISITING THE FOX, the Little Prince went to a deserted place and there he stayed wrapped in thought. It was a rocky, desolate and lonely place where he could see for miles, but for miles there was nothing to be seen, just towering peaks shaped like needles. He didn't eat or drink for a long time such was his preoccupation with what his friend the fox had said.

Then one day he climbed a peak and called out into the wilderness. Instead of an echo he heard a voice reply:

"If you have a powerful spirit within you that can make you happy, why doesn't it feed you? Why doesn't it take away your thirst?"

But the Little Prince understood that his body was just a shell, a heavy garment, his outward appearance. What was important could not be seen. What it wanted could and should be disregarded.

He called out again and heard another voice:

THE GOSPEL ACCORDING TO SAINT X

"If you can disregard your shell then why not get rid of it, like a snake shuffles off its skin?"'

And the Little Prince thought about how appealing that was. To live just as a pure spirit without the body that seemed to want so many needless things. But he understood that his body was necessary, at least for a while and he could not leave it just yet.

Again, he called out and heard the reply:

"If this body is needed by the spirit, you must listen to it and fulfil all that it desires."

But the Little Prince understood that it is the invisible in him that is the master of the visible. He saw that people who prioritise material things can never be at peace or be happy. In fact, their comforts make them slaves.

He understood that his real father, the one he should obey, was the source of this spirit. His father's will was embodied in it. It was the voice inside him that only he could hear, and it was his heart not his head that told the truth. If he could listen to his heart and not to others or his body, he could be truly at peace and be happy. Not only that, but he could also show others how to be happy too.

He called out again *"God is the spirit in man."*

And he heard the wilderness reply.

"God is the spirit in man."

After that the Little Prince left the wild and rocky place and went to say hello again to his friend the fox. The fox was very pleased to see him and immediately noticed a change.

When they parted, the fox said, "the Little Prince will be the saviour of everyone."

*****

Hearing this, a pilot who had also come to listen to the fox, decided to follow the Little Prince and listen to what he had to say.

The pilot had become very lost despite studying geography for many, many years. He could easily tell Kansas from China, from high in the sky in his plane, but there seemed to be no maps for people who had become as lost as he had become. He felt that once he understood the world but no longer. Once he had wanted to be a painter, but receiving no praise for his work he left it for other things. He studied geography, history, arithmetic, and grammar. He had changed his behaviour to be like other people and had stopped listening to himself. He felt that something was broken and that he lacked the tools to fix it. He was looking for a teacher that could tell him what had gone wrong.

But at first the pilot wasn't sure. How could this funny little man have the answers he sought? He wore rags and looked like he had just stepped out of the wilderness.

BOB PROPHETTE

It's easy for grown-ups to be confused by appearances.

But when he listened to the Little Prince, he was very moved by what he heard and he resolved to be his companion, to follow him, learn what he could, and help him.

The Little Prince was very happy. He knew the pilot could be helpful. The pilot could take him anywhere.

And so, the pilot and the Little Prince boarded the plane, took off and began their journey.

THE GOSPEL ACCORDING TO SAINT X

Chapter Three

THE FIRST PLANET they came to was inhabited by an old gentleman surrounded by a large quantity of voluminous books. He was dressed with impressive style and elegance.

"Ah", he said with a broad smile, "here comes a reader."

"Please, what are you doing here?" asked the Little Prince.

"I am a librarian," said the man. "I keep the books in order. I am accurate."

"And what is in the books?" asked the Little Prince. "Do they contain poems?"

"That, I could not tell you," replied the librarian.

"Do they have stories about wise people?"

"I could not tell you that either. People order words to make books, I order books to make a library. I administrate them. I know the title of every book, I make a note of it, give it a number and put it in the correct place. In order. Would you like to read one?" The librarian said, and he

handed the Little Prince a very large dusty book, too heavy to lift from the floor.

"And, if you please,'" went on the Little Prince, "how do people know what is in the books?"

"I can't help you there, I'm afraid. I am accurate."

The Little Prince began to read. To his surprise he found everything he had learned was already in the book. In the book, it was clearly written 'The spirit of God is in you.'

"That's funny," said the Little Prince. "That's exactly what I learned from the fox."

Puzzled, he said to the pilot, "everything I can teach you is already here."

"My dear little fellow," said the pilot, "that's not how it works at all. Just because it's written in a book doesn't mean people will understand it. Most people are like this librarian, they know *of* books, sometimes they *read* them, less often they *understand* them…and there are many, many books."

Closing his book with a lofty air, the librarian said "and that is why a Librarian is the most important person. I haven't time to read the books. I'm too busy finding where to put them. I leave the reading to others."

"And does anyone read them?" asked the Little Prince, "and how do people know which books to read and how to understand them?"

"No" said the librarian, "sadly I get very few readers here I am afraid. As for understanding…you should speak to the Lamplighters. They are everywhere, you should have no trouble finding one."

And the Little Prince understood. He laid the book carefully on the ground and the pilot and librarian waited for what he would say.

"Well" said the Little Prince, "I think I know what the books say. And I'm going to show people what they mean."

Chapter Four

SAYING THEIR GOODBYES to the librarian, the pilot and the Little Prince walked out into the fields beside the library. The fields were like a sea full of corn. As they had become very hungry the pilot plucked some corn, rubbed it in his hands and began to eat the kernels.

"Try this" said the pilot, "it's good and will keep us going."

A man with a lamp noticed them and rushed up saying "Can't you see that my lamp is unlit, and don't you know it's Saturday? You cannot work on a Saturday, and I just saw you rubbing those ears of corn."

The Little Prince saluted the lamplighter respectfully. He liked lamps and wondered if the lamplighter would light his lamp and make things nice and jolly. Lanterns reminded the Little Prince of stars and sunsets, which are some of the nicest things to be reminded of. But by the expression on the man's face, the Prince was worried he had offended him.

THE GOSPEL ACCORDING TO SAINT X

"Please, where does it say you cannot work on a Saturday?" asked the Prince, giving the lamplighter a courteous salute and a gentle bow.

"In the book" replied the lamplighter. "The lamps not lit. As you can see. My orders are to extinguish the lamp on Saturday so everyone knows what they can and cannot do. The punishment is death."

"Death!" exclaimed the Little Prince. 'But don't the people already know what they should and shouldn't be doing?"

"The lamp's unlit, those are my orders" said the lamplighter. "If I don't tell them, who knows what they would do?"

"We have just come from your library and I read that it said *love is more important than sacrifice.*"

"The book also says, work on Saturday and you die. The lamp's unlit. Those are my orders."

"But that's a contradiction" said the Little Prince. "You can't very well love people if you go around killing them because of something you read in a book."

"Those are my orders" repeated the lamplighter, taking out a checkered handkerchief to wipe his brow. "They keep me very busy. The time was when hardly anyone needed reminding, but now that's changed. The lamp's unlit.'

"What a funny man you are" said the Little Prince. "I like your lamp but I don't think you are using it well."

Further on the pilot and the Little Prince came across a woman who was struggling with a heavy load. The Little Prince began to help her.

THE GOSPEL ACCORDING TO SAINT X

And again, a lamplighter appeared saying "The lamp's unlit. It's Saturday, you should not be doing that. Those are my orders."

The Little Prince ignored him, thinking what a strange planet we are on. It's full of books which no-one reads and yet full of people telling you what you should and shouldn't do.

Turning to the pilot the Little Prince said, "I think this lamplighter is a little absurd. He is deceiving himself. He takes things from a book without understanding it and uses it against others. He's mixed everything up. He's confused and confusing others."

"Just so" said the pilot. "I know this planet well. I crash landed here one time. Took me a long time to get the right parts. They don't like people like me because I don't do what they say. I can take you to meet some people I met last time. One is a collector of taxes, the other buys and sells, and the last one… well…he gives men what they desire."

"Yes, I'd like that" said the Little Prince.

When they arrived at the place the pilot mentioned, they saw three similar people, sat at three similar desks, wearing three similar hats. Each hat had a label. The first said Tax. The second said Stuff and the last said Desire.

BOB PROPHETTE

The Little Prince introduced himself politely and asked of the first "Why do you collect taxes?"

"I don't know, it's my job." And after a pause, "Taxes are necessary to build roads and houses so that people can get what they desire."

"And if you please, why do you buy and sell?" asked the Little Prince of the other.

"I never thought about it. I guess because people want things. There are lots of people and they want many things" he replied. "Besides, I have to pay taxes."

"And why do you give men what they desire?" asked the Little Prince of the third, who he could see, unlike the others, had painted his face to be more jolly.

"So that I have money to buy things from the merchant and pay my taxes" was the reply.

That's all very curious, thought the Little Prince. They think in circles, each larger than the next. He was beginning to understand why the pilot had become so lost.

And so, the pilot and the Little Prince went into the house of the tax collector and his friends. The hosts were very kind and showed them lots of hospitality.

They asked the Little Prince many questions and he was pleased that they listened to his views.

Outside in the street some lamplighters had gathered. They spoke among themselves and were very confused as to why this newcomer, the Little Prince, would want to associate himself with such people.

"Why doesn't he talk to us?" they said. "After all we are the lamplighters. We know what is right and what is wrong."

But the Little Prince was beginning to realise that there was no point trying to talk to lamplighters. They already thought they knew and yet they didn't. They reasoned in the smallest circle of all.

BOB PROPHETTE

Better I talk with people like my pilot's friends, thought the Little Prince. They are confused but know they have something to learn. The others won't hear what I say anyway. What I say will be heard by those who need to hear and ignored by those who don't. People are funny that way.

But the lamplighters continued to harass the Little Prince.

"You're sitting wrong."

"You shouldn't eat that."

"You can't say that."

And so on and so on.

Taking pity on the lamplighters, the Little Prince tried one more time.

"Everything you tell people is contradictory" he said. "How do you expect anyone to listen to what you say?"

"But these are the orders" replied the lamplighters.

It is as if the wisdom of the wise has been lost and the understanding of the thinkers has been dimmed, thought the Little Prince.

"Maybe your orders made sense once, but you have lost sight of why, and you are using your lamps wrongly. Don't you know that what you order people to do must make sense?" said the Little Prince. "Every King understands that.

You are doing things for no other reason than you have been told to. What if you had been told something else? You would do otherwise. Isn't it better to listen to the voice inside you?"

When one of the lamplighters said that the Little Prince had become dirty because he ate dirty things and associated with dirty people, the Prince said "On my planet there is a rose. It is very beautiful. I give it fresh water and make sure it has enough light and air. There is nothing wrong with the things I give it and yet it is vain and unkind to me.

"I think" continued the Little Prince, "that there is nothing that can happen to anyone that makes them bad. What makes them bad is what they do to others."

Later, when they were alone the pilot said "Look here my little man, I'm not sure I understand what you meant. Can you say it more plainly?"

The Little Prince sat in contemplation for a moment and then said "Don't you see, if these people think in circles they will never go anywhere. If only they listened to the voice inside them! But that's the voice that's the quietest of all. It's just as the fox said."

"Indeed" said the pilot. "I think I can sometimes hardly hear the voice myself."

BOB PROPHETTE

"You need to listen more carefully" said the Little Prince. "Perhaps it's time we left this planet."

THE GOSPEL ACCORDING TO SAINT X

Chapter Five

THE NEXT PLANET the pair came to was even stranger than the last. On it was a large temple and in the temple were many people, many cows, sheep and doves. Soldiers with guns stood around the temple entrance looking very glum and making sure everyone was scared of them.

Inside the temple, sat behind a desk too small for his bulk, was a man counting. He was so busy he didn't even look up when the Little Prince and the pilot came inside.

"Two thousand three hundred and forty-four thefts, that's forty-two cows, eight sheep and twenty doves."

"Eight million four hundred and forty-four blasphemies, that's two hundred and eighty-five sheep and three thousand doves."

Puzzled, the Little Prince asked "Please, what are you doing?"

Ignored, he asked again. "Please, what are you doing?"

"What?" said the man. "An interruption! Humph. Can't you see I am busy?"

"Please, I can see you are busy, but can you tell me what you are busy doing?"

"Reckoning" came the reply.

"Reckoning what?" asked the Prince.

"Reckoning the debts. You are in the house of our God, it is here you can come to make amends for the things you have done wrong. Lamplighters tell me who has done what to whom, I count up all the things that people have done wrong and I tell them how much they have to pay. It's very time consuming. It's a serious business and I'm a very busy man."

"But..." replied the Little Prince, "don't people already know what they have done wrong? If they already know and they are sorry, why do you make them pay?"

"But if they don't pay, then there will be no money for the temple" came the reply.

"But a temple is just lumps of rock" said the Prince. "Think of all the happiness there would be if everyone knew that as long as they acted better, everything was forgiven. Then they wouldn't do the wrong thing and have to give you money for more bricks."

"Can't you see I'm too busy to do that?" replied the man.

The Little Prince continued "If the temple is something that is meant to help people be at peace and be happy, then surely being kind and doing the right thing can be a temple too? Then you won't need so many bricks."

"Five hundred and three murders, that's fifteen thousand and eight cows" went on the man behind the desk.

It's quite possible this man is absurd, thought the Little Prince.

"You are ridiculous" said the Prince crossly. He untied the rope which held the cows, sheep and doves so they could be let loose. This made the man in the temple very angry. His face became even redder than before.

"Soldiers!" he cried out.

"Time to go!" said the pilot, and they left.

But many people heard what the Little Prince had done and started to question what they had been told before.

Chapter Six

FURTHER ON IN THEIR JOURNEY they came to a very dry place. It was inhabited by just two people, who didn't seem to have enough water. One was tall, dressed in style and elegance and seemed to think very highly of himself indeed. The other was smaller and dressed in rags.

The two people would have nothing to do with one another except that they had to share a well which was almost always dry. The well sat on a rocky out-crop surrounded by dusty yellow rocks.

The well-dressed man was drawing water and the Little Prince said "Please sir, may we have some water?"

"What?" asked the man, "I don't share water with other people. Never have and never will."

"And does that make you happy?" asked the Little Prince, "or any less thirsty?"

"Happy?" said the rich man. "No, I don't suppose it does and I am always thirsty. But I'm not about to change the way I act because some little man asks me for water. You have your ways I have mine."

Meanwhile the pilot, remembering that he had some pills that stop you becoming dehydrated gave them to the man dressed in rags, saying "I will give you more, but you must share them with the rich man. They're magic."

The man in rags did as he was told, offering the rich man exactly half of all the pills the pilot had given him. The rich man was very moved by this. So much so that the Little Prince was sure, had he not been so dehydrated, he might have shed a tear of joy.

* * * * *

That evening after they had found somewhere to rest, the pilot thought a lot about the Little Prince and his friend the fox and what they had said.

They are very similar he thought. Each of them attends carefully and listens to the voice inside them and is guided by it to do the right thing. Neither of them listens to what others say, whether it is right or wrong. They seem to know that they have already been born with this knowledge inside them and listening to that voice is always the right thing to do.

Turning to the Little Prince who had fallen asleep, he whispered "I'm beginning to know what you mean about God being the spirit in man."

* * * * *

Continuing their journey, the pair again came across a group of lamplighters, who invited them to dinner. The lamplighters continued to be puzzled and perplexed by the

Little Prince and wanted to ask him more questions as they found it hard to understand what he was saying.

Other people on the planet heard and saw what the Little Prince said and did, and were beginning to think there may be another way. They were very moved and knew the Little Prince was special. They felt that he had come to save them from the stupid lamplighters and their rules. Although few said anything, most ordinary people thought that was a very good thing indeed.

At dinner, before they had begun to eat, a poor woman came to the Little Prince. She was very pleased to see him.

"Hello" said the Little Prince.

Without saying a word, she sat at his feet and began to cry. The land of tears is such a sad place, thought the Little Prince and he tried to comfort her. But she cried so much she had to wipe his feet dry with her hair and later took a bottle of perfume, her prized possession, and poured it over his feet to freshen them.

"That tickles!" giggled the Little Prince, breaking out in a lovely peel of laughter.

How funny these people are, he thought. He was very moved by the woman's actions, and he smiled kindly at her, pleased to see how happy her actions made her.

BOB PROPHETTE

The Little Prince could see that his host the lamplighter thought it was wrong that the woman should be doing this. His face was curled in disapproval. She was just a poor woman and the perfume was inexpensive. He couldn't understand why the Little Prince would be so pleased. He, a lamplighter, had invited the Prince into his home and offered him luxury, yet the Little Prince had not so much as smiled at him.

"You know" said the Little Prince, "I once met a man who had two friends, both of whom owed him money. One owed him a lot and the other very little. He forgave them both. I think you and this woman are like that man's friends. You have a lot of things and think you know what is right, she has very little and knows she has much to learn. Look how she attends to me. She has shown me a great deal of love and you have merely been polite. That is why I smiled at her. You think you know everything already and so you cannot show me love as she does.

"You remind me" chuckled the Little Prince, "of the conceited man I met on Asteroid 326.

"He wanted to be regarded as the handsomest, the best-dressed, the richest, and the most intelligent man on his planet. He even had a hat which he wore especially so he could salute his admirers when they applauded him.

"I thought he was very silly indeed."

"It seemed to me" continued the Little Prince, "that by thinking himself to be better than others, he just made himself worse."

"But this woman" said the lamplighter, "she follows none of the rules. She does all the things she shouldn't do. Should she be allowed to run around happy as a child?

BOB PROPHETTE

That's not right. She should be sorry for the things she has done wrong and work hard to make amends."

"Why should she feel bad?" asked the Little Prince. "What a funny man you are lamplighter! The reason she feels happy" continued the Little Prince, "is that she acts out of love and humility, putting others first rather than herself.

"If she went around being sorry all the time for breaking your rules, she wouldn't be able to show all that love, would she? I'm telling you something that you know but have forgotten. When you remember it, you won't need your old rules. It is your rules that should be forgotten."

*****

"It's like a part that's worn out on my plane" said the pilot sometime later, "sometimes it just cannot be repaired."

"Exactly so" agreed the Little Prince.

"Do you think these people can really change?" went on the pilot. "Do you think that's possible?"

"Some of them" said the Little Prince, "Not everyone."

THE GOSPEL ACCORDING TO SAINT X

Chapter Seven

LEAVING THE PLANET of the lamplighters the pilot used the time to ask the Little Prince some more questions. He wondered whether the things the Little Prince taught were really the same as those of his odd little friend the fox.

"Yes" said the Little Prince, "the fox and I are saying very much the same thing."

"If that is the case" the pilot asked, "why haven't people listened to the fox before?"

"Not everyone is able to hear when a fox speaks to them" replied the Prince. "Some people can only hear the things said by people like themselves.

"Some people will not hear me when I speak" continued the Little Prince.

THE GOSPEL ACCORDING TO SAINT X

"Like the astronomer! The one who discovered your planet?" suggested the pilot. "No one listened to his discovery until he dressed the same way as his audience. Then they all listened attentively."

"Exactly!" exclaimed the Little Prince. "If he had not changed his clothes, no-one would even believe in the existence of my planet. But the fox's discovery is far more important than that of the astronomer."

"*The kingdom of God is at hand*, you mean?" asked the pilot. "I wanted to ask you what that means."

"It means it is here, there and everywhere. It has neither time nor place" answered the Little Prince, "because it is inside everyone already."

"But how can a kingdom be inside people?" asked the pilot with a look of puzzlement.

The Little Prince lay down on the ground to give some thought as to how best he could explain this to the pilot. He could see he was having some difficulty understanding, even though he really wanted to.

He stared at the flowers that were all around him and then said "I think when you are born, something is given to you, the Spirit. It's more than the flesh in which it resides and can last forever."

"Even though we die?" asked the pilot.

"Even though we die" replied the Prince.

"This Spirit is pure and tells us what to do if we listen carefully enough. It is that Spirit that has continued as men's bodies have come and passed away. But as men grow, they stop hearing the voice and become preoccupied with other things. They stop listening and think they need rules to govern them and those around them. But the Spirit is telling them what they should do. It's the voice in your head. It's

more important than rules. If you pay close attention it can guide you in any situation. Rules can never do that. Sometimes rules work, but mostly they don't. Everyone can feel the spirit within them. It is something which lives in freedom and reason. If men are not free and do not use their reason, it cannot thrive" explained the Prince.

"I'm still not sure I understand" said the pilot.

"It's not really a mystery that is hard to figure out" said the Little Prince. "Many people will tell you that there is a God who is somehow outside them, and Heaven is a place they may visit after they have died."

"Yes" agreed the pilot, "many people seem to believe that."

"How can they believe such a thing, but not believe in what is inside themselves? Something they can actually feel and listen to, something they recognise instantly in others. Is it really that difficult to understand? No-one goes to Heaven to meet God" continued the Little Prince. "They find God in themselves, if they look. And they can create a Heaven here, through how they act towards others.

"If they find this Spirit they will be at peace with the world and with themselves and, because it is what they are supposed to do, they can help others see how they should act and in that way the Spirit in man will never end. It keeps growing.

BOB PROPHETTE

"But if they do not find this peace, if they do not listen to that voice inside them, then when the body dies, the Spirit dies with them. The Spirit is like a light. You remember on my planet" went on the Little Prince, "when I wanted to grow some grass so that I could sit on it and enjoy the sunsets?"

"Yes" said the pilot.

"I threw the seed everywhere I could. Some seeds fell into the extinct volcano and didn't have a chance to grow. Other seeds fell into the active volcanoes and were burned up. Yet others fell where there were baobab seeds and could not survive as the baobabs sprouted. But some of the seeds fell on good soil. The seed that fell on the good soil grew and so I had grass on which I could sit and watch the sunsets which I like very much.

"Or when I make my breakfast, I mix the yeast, water and flour and leave the dough next to one of my active volcanoes. They are very useful for making bread rise."

"I'm still not sure what you mean about the seeds" said the pilot. "Are the seeds the Spirit?"

"No!" laughed the Little Prince. "Think of the seeds as what the fox and I are telling and showing you. It may be heard and seen by some people, but those people are too hard and dead for it to make any difference. That's the seed that reaches the extinct volcano. The teaching may be heard and accepted for a time, but then wither away because they landed on the slopes of the active volcano. These are the people who accept the teaching for a while but give it up when things get difficult.

"The teaching that reaches the soil where the baobab seeds lie, represents the people who are open to temptation by all the worldly things in life, the distractions. The teaching makes no difference because the baobab trees eventually take over. This is the most dangerous thing, since they may take over and destroy the planet. If the baobab trees can be taken care of, then I will have a very nice planet, and many creatures can live happily there, including me. You remember what happens when the baobab seeds are not resisted?" asked the Prince.

"Yes" said the pilot, "I remember I made that drawing. You said my baobab trees looked like cabbages, cabbages that can destroy a planet!"

THE GOSPEL ACCORDING TO SAINT X

"Just so" the Little Prince laughed, "and that is why I wanted to have a sheep. Even a little lamb can eat the baobabs when they are still small. Sheep are very useful for that."

Chapter Eight

THE PILOT AND THE Little Prince decided to return to the Little Prince's planet and were surprised to find a lot of people waiting for them, so many in fact that the Little Prince was worried they would damage his planet. It was after all, very small. But the Little Prince had become very popular, and many people wanted to hear what he had to say.

"I think you should talk to them," said the pilot. "Climb up by that extinct volcano so that everyone can hear you."

"Ok" said the Little Prince, "but keep an eye out because you never can tell."

Although the volcano barely came up to his knees it was just enough for him to be seen.

He began.

"If…" he started hesitantly, then with more confidence as he saw the smiling faces in front of him, he continued "If you are poor and have few things, don't worry. Having lots of things is a nuisance and a distraction from all that's good about life."

"Ahhh!" Said the crowd.

Encouraged by the crowd's reaction, he went on.

"And don't worry if others look down on you, by doing so they make themselves below you. They themselves are ridiculous.

"I once knew a man who thought himself very rich. He took things everyone thought belonged to all and called them his own. In reality he had nothing of value and so always wanted more. This was a 'serious business for him' and he was 'a busy man.'

"I think he was very silly" said the Prince.

"Ohhh!" exclaimed the crowd.

BOB PROPHETTE

"I also knew a man who only wanted to be praised and admired for no reason other than he liked applause. He was very silly indeed."

The crowd laughed.

"People who have nothing, have many things to teach those who have much. They should not be afraid or embarrassed to say so."

The crowd cheered.

Some of those who had come to listen wanted to ask questions. Many were still confused by what the Little Prince had said on the planet of the lamplighters.

"Do you not think people should follow the rules?" one woman asked.

"Not for the sake of it, without questioning why" replied the Little Prince. "The rules must make sense to you. If you cannot say why you are following a rule, I think you should not bother yourself to follow it," he continued.

"If the best you can say of yourself is that '*I did what I was told to do*' you have little to be happy about."

"Do you have any rules?" asked another.

"Please, don't misunderstand me. Rules in themselves are not bad, it's following them without thinking that gets you into trouble. It's better to do what feels to be right, listen to your heart and use your own judgement."

The Little Prince could see his audience were still unsure.

"Look, if you write a rule in the sand here, I can tell you what I think about it."

One of the listeners picked up a stick and wrote

"You should not kill."

"Kill!" said the Little Prince, 'isn't that obvious to you? I think that's a very silly rule to have. Why do you think you even need such a rule? I say you should not even get angry in the first place.

"Everyday, before you do anything else, ask if you have upset someone and if you have, go and make peace with them, immediately. Do this and you won't need any rules about killing!"

He could see the crowd agreeing.

Another listener picked up the stick and wrote

"You should not cheat on your wife."

"I say you are responsible for what you love, the people and things you tame" said the Little Prince. "Two people who have tamed each other should look after each other. That is the price of the happiness that taming brings.

BOB PROPHETTE

"A partner is your lover and your friend and real friendship is forever. It is better that you do not tame someone, than tame them and then reject them.

"People are not things that you can abandon when they are no longer useful. Rejecting someone you have tamed only creates problems for everyone. The rejected seek others and tempt those others to reject yet more others. It's a circle of hurt and misery."

And another wrote

"Don't use God's name to swear a lie."

'I say, do not promise anything. You can never know what will happen, so what is a promise? If a promise is fulfilled it would have been so, had you not promised. If it isn't fulfilled then you have misled another. Promises are either obviously things that will happen or they are lies. At every point be guided to do what you think is right and let be what will be."

Another wrote

"Match the punishment to the crime."

"I say" said the Little Prince "you should not judge and even if you do, you cannot fight evil with evil. Evil can only be defeated by good.

"Adding evil to evil just makes more evil."

He continued, "If someone hurts you, do not judge them. Perhaps the harm they do you is the lesser of that harm that might otherwise befall you both. Most people who do harm have been harmed themselves. Instead act with kindness. Then there will be no punishment and the cycle of evil will be broken."

Another said,

"Love your neighbour."

"I say" said the Little Prince, "everyone, no matter what planet they are from, is your neighbour. Make no distinction between you and anyone else, because you are all the same. Act in kindness to everyone, no matter how different you think you are."

After a pause the Little Prince restated his rules,

"If you look inside yourself, you will not need any rules, but if you must have rules, these are what I suggest:

1. Do not be angry and if you are make amends quickly.
2. Act responsibly towards the things you have tamed.
3. Do not mislead by making promises, just do.
4. Do not fight evil with evil or judge others.
5. Treat everyone alike.

"In following these rules, if you ever get confused, remember one thing: all that you wish men to do to you, do yourself to them. Do these things because you know they are right, not because you have been told to. If you act like this, you will find peace and you will not need the praise of other people."

"What if we forget these new rules?" asked one of the crowd after a pause.

The Little Prince chuckled, "well, there aren't many to remember, but to remind you of the way you should behave. you might repeat to yourself the following, so that you do not easily forget:

Dear Infinite,
You are the source, my father.
I know you with my Heart. You are amazing!
Everything, including me, comes from you and I will do what I know to be right.
You give everything I need to be at peace.
If I act wrongly, I will change. And I will forgive others quickly if they do wrong to me.
Because dear Infinite, you are amazing!

"Remember this… If the lamplighters tell you to do what would be bad for yourself, or prevent you from being kind to others, then you know you should not listen to them."

*****

THE GOSPEL ACCORDING TO SAINT X

Many of those who listened to what the Little Prince said were quite amazed. His rules made so much sense they hardly needed to remember them. In fact, they weren't really rules at all, but how they would behave if they were free and lived in reason.

Chapter Nine

AS THE LITTLE PRINCE'S PLANET had by now become very crowded indeed, they decided to take a trip. "I know of a planet that has a lovely swimming pool with some interesting history" said the pilot.

"That sounds nice" said the Little Prince, "perhaps we can go swimming and you can tell me the story."

And so, they set off for the planet with the miraculous pool. When they arrived, the pilot told him the story.

"As I understand it, this pool is usually very quiet and calm, but sometimes it bubbles. They say that the bubbles are the result of a genie who stirs up the water from time to time."

"How funny" smiled the Little Prince.

"Anyone who enters the water while it is bubbling will be cured of any illness they have" said the pilot.

"Huh!" said the Little Prince. 'Is there medicine in the water?"

"I don't think so," said the pilot. "From what geography I was taught in school, I think it's probably some air from the rocks below that makes the bubbles.'

With a mischievous grin the Little Prince looked over at the pilot and said "shall we play a game?"

The pilot nodded.

"If there is no medicine in the water, the people are probably not sick anyway. Maybe it's just in their heads. People can convince themselves of the strangest things."

"Indeed" agreed the pilot.

"People have started to believe in me and what I say. Perhaps if I tell them they are cured, that will have the same effect?"

The pair decided to see if this would work on an old man who lay on a mat some distance from the swimming pool. The Little Prince approached him.

"Please sir, what seems to be the matter?"

"I'm waiting for the water to bubble so that I can get in. I've been here many years but as I am so old and weak, I never seem to be able to get to the pool in time, others always get there before me. I do like bubbles. It's a very bad shame I cannot reach them, try as I might."

"Well, I am the Little Prince. Do you know me?" Asked the Prince.

"Yes" nodded the man. "People say you are very special."

The Little Prince put his hand solemnly on the man's shoulders. "I say you are cured. Go now and live your life as others do."

And the old man, feeling better, collected his things and walked happily off. That is until he came across a lamplighter who told him it was Saturday, and he shouldn't be carrying anything anywhere.

But the old man ignored him and said it was OK because the Little Prince had said so.

This made the lamplighter quite annoyed.

As they left that planet, the pilot asked the Little Prince: "Is it enough that people don't break your rules, will they then be happy?"

"No" said the Little Prince. "It's better that people actually do good things, rather than just not doing bad things or following rules.

"It's like this" he said, "imagine there is a ruler of a planet, and he has ten subjects. He gives each of them a gold coin. Now some of his subjects take the coin and through effort earn more coins with it on behalf of the ruler. Others do nothing, deciding just to return the coin to the ruler when he asks for it back.

"What do you think the ruler should do?" asked the Little Prince.

"He should be grateful to the ones who had earned more and annoyed with the ones who had done nothing" said the pilot.

"Exactly! Next time he goes away he would probably give all the money to those who used it well" said the Little Prince, "and so it is with your time. It's better to use it to make everyone better off, than not.

"Those that use it well will be happier and the Spirit will thrive in them. Those that don't use it well will receive nothing in return."

*****

Another time, the Little Prince and the pilot were again with a large crowd of people who had come to listen and ask questions.

It was time to eat but the Little Prince saw that while some had brought lots of food, others had brought none at all. So, he told the pilot to share some of their food with the others and pretty soon everyone was sharing out so that no one went hungry, even those that had brought nothing. In fact, after sharing out what everyone had, there was even some left over!

Pretty soon a group of lamplighters got together, and they began to complain about the way the Little Prince was acting. They wondered if he was a bad person for not following the rules, even though what he said always seemed very sensible and those that listened to him seemed to be happier.

THE GOSPEL ACCORDING TO SAINT X

no one could happen to do it, so that had brought nothing. In fact, after changing his initial views of had, there was no saying left in it.

They soon a group of he might-boys not together, and they began to complain about the way the kind. Phineas was saying. They wondered if he was a happiness for me, of following the rules, even though when he said always seemed more sensible, and those that attracted to him seemed of his ways happier.

Chapter Ten

GIVEN THE UNUSUAL NATURE of his birth it is perhaps not surprising that the Little Prince wasn't like a normal son to his 'parents'. It was not that he did not love his family, he did. It was just that he loved everybody else too and he could see that some people thought it was enough to love their family and didn't need to love anyone else.

The love he felt for others made him very popular and many people wanted to follow him and be part of his 'family'. This made the Little Prince chuckle.

"Where do you think they want to go to with me?" he asked the pilot. "My planet is very small!"

One man wanted to live in the same way as the Little Prince but said he must bury his dead father first. The Little Prince thought this funny too.

"Why do they worry about who will bury their dead shells? I can see they don't really understand the difference between flesh and spirit."

He thought the same of all those who said that they wanted to change but just had to do something else first, before they could start. The Little Prince was sure that these people had just not understood.

However, another time he came across two sisters. One wanted to listen to what the Little Prince had to say, while the other was busy, rushing around, making meals and taking care of the house. The Little Prince could see that the flesh had a very strong control on some people and he wondered how he could help them break free.

He told the busy sister, "I know you expect me to be grateful to you for all your work, and I am, but I am more grateful that your sister is taking time to listen. You are so busy I don't think you spend enough time reflecting on how you can be a better person. You do something for me and forget to attend to yourself. I know it's confusing but helping others can be a distraction if we haven't first helped ourselves to be a better person. Do you see what I mean? You think you have lots of time to do both, but it's not true."

He told them again the story of the businessman who was very busy counting stars. This time he told them that just as the businessman had counted his 6th millionth star, the next star he counted was one that came crashing into his planet destroying him and all his ledgers.

He asked them to think about this.

"What is sad about this story? That the businessman never got to count any more stars? Or that he never had time to realise how foolish he was being, change his life and do good for others?"

He continued "don't put off changing your ways because at any moment it may be too late.

"This is not difficult to understand" said the Little Prince, "many things are uncertain but one thing that is not is that we all will eventually die. The saddest thing is to die before you have found peace. You should be willing to give up everything to find that peace. Especially silly things like counting stars."

A man came to the Little Prince and asked "what if I give up all the material things in life, live as you do, and I don't find peace?"

"You are like those people on the trains" said the Little Prince, "busy people in bundles of 1000 going from here to there, never satisfied, pursuing nothing at all. They miss everything around them. Only the children seemed to understand, only the children have time to look out the windows and enjoy the ride. Only children see with their hearts. The children follow the will of their true fathers, while their fathers themselves are lost."

The Little Prince was by now getting a little frustrated.

'Why is it so difficult to understand?" asked the Little Prince. "In matters of the flesh everyone seems to understand how to increase their wealth, but in the matters of the Spirit, no-one seems to understand anything."

Perhaps it was time for another story, thought the Little Prince.

"I once met a man who I thought was very sad indeed. He was a drunk. He had very cleverly found a way of making his drunkenness make sense to himself. When I asked him why he drank, he said

"*I drink to forget, to forget I am ashamed, ashamed that I drink.*'

"How cleverly we act to justify our bad behaviours! I only wish some of you used your cleverness to find the peace I am talking about!"

A man came to the Little Prince and said "I do not know what you mean by the *true Father's will*. Can you please explain it to me?"

BOB PROPHETTE

"I didn't have a fleshy father and in that I feel more fortunate than you because it meant that I could see that my true father, all our fathers, is the universe.

"Ask yourself who your father is, and who his father is, and then his...keep going and ultimately you will see that your father must be the universe, because it's the oldest thing that there is.

"Fleshy fathers teach their sons how to get along in the world, how to accumulate riches, how to make their flesh comfortable. But there can be no happiness in this. Sons listen to their fleshy fathers and stop thinking for themselves. Neither are they free, their riches are heavy things that they must carry around with them.

"If I brought before you my rose, the Lazy Man, the King, the Drunkard, the Conceited Man, the Businessman, the Geographer, the Pill-peddler, the Switchman...the Lamplighter...all the people I have told you about...Do you think that a world composed of these people is what the universe intended for us? Only the fox seemed to know, even though it is already written down in your books which no one reads."

"Can you please bring the fox to us so that we can hear him?" asked the man.

"I cannot" stated the Prince. "In any case, unless you already understand you will not be able to hear him. No-one can teach you what you already know. You want too much to be like the Lazy Man, the King, the Drunkard, etc. Until you have given up wanting those things you cannot have peace. The fox knows this and would be willing to chew through his paw to be free. If people carry on this way there will be no everlasting life. Humanity will be destroyed. The light that is inside you and shines in the universe will be extinguished.

"Imagine if my pilot here could take us in his airplane off into the future. But not one future, two. In the first, everyone learned to listen to what the fox is saying, to listen to themselves and make peace with the universe. In the second no one listened, and they just carried on as usual.

"In the first future there would be a universe filled with happy people. In the other, if anyone survives at all, it will be just as it is now or worse. This is the choice you have to make.

"I cannot take you on that plane to convince you, it is not possible, but that's what it would look like. Those happy people in the future cannot come to speak to you and neither can the unhappy ones. Even if they could come, I am not sure you would listen. I am sure those future happy people would want to come and tell you themselves. But in a way they are already here, as they would say the same things as the voice inside you."

A rich man came before the Little Prince and said "I like very much what you are saying. I have listened to your rules, and I will follow them."

The Little Prince looked at his expensive clothes and raised one eyebrow. "Will you continue to dress that way, wrapped in fine clothes while others have little? If you do, you haven't really heard what I have said."

The rich man frowned and went away as he didn't want to give up his nice clothes.

The Little Prince sighed.

What the Prince said made many of those who had come to listen uncomfortable. But the Little Prince continued "It makes you uncomfortable because you know it is true. You cannot be rich and be happy when others are in need. It would be easier for my pilot to fly his plane through the eye of a needle than for a rich man to be at peace with himself, though he may make his flesh very comfortable indeed."

THE GOSPEL ACCORDING TO SAINT X

He went on "it would be easier to keep ten elephants on my planet than continue to have so much, when others have so little."

The Little Prince saw some small children by a tree and told the crowd to go and observe how they played together. One of the children had taken all the toys for himself. Some of the crowd thought it silly that they should be watching children play, but the Little Prince just said "watch…!"

The child with many toys looked lonely. As he had taken all the toys for himself, he had no one to play with. He looked embarrassed as he sat there alone surrounded by toys. Then he rose and gave one of the toys to a child sat near him and they began to play together.

"See how the child is happier now because he has shared?"'

Then the child who had been given the toy passed it to another child who had nothing. The crowd were surprised to see the second child happier than the first.

And the Little Prince said "herein is the whole story. The first child knew he would be happier if he shared with the others. He had many toys and they had none, but this second child gave away his only toy and he is happier still because of the good deed he has done. A deed much more significant than that of the first child, because he had nothing. Act like this second child and then you will be happy."

And the crowd began to talk about what they had seen. Many seemed to understand and discussed examples of ways in which they could make themselves and others happier by doing good to one another. They talked and talked with one another, becoming ever more excited by the new ideas. And the Little Prince looked glumly at them and said a little crossly "so why are you still standing here discussing what you have seen? Those in need are all around you."

THE GOSPEL ACCORDING TO SAINT X

Chapter Eleven

MANY OF THE LAMPLIGHTERS continued to be angry with the Little Prince and could not understand why so many listened to him and not them. They could see he was a problem.

As the Little Prince and the pilot continued their travels it seemed that whatever they did they could not help but upset another lamplighter somewhere, they had so many rules.

One lamplighter was angry that the Little Prince was late to a festival even though the time had been clearly announced. Others didn't like that he was always doing good deeds when he shouldn't be. But the thing they liked the least was that he didn't believe their lamps were necessary and neither their temples. The lamplighters liked their lamps and their temples very much.

Many of them were confused by the Little Prince's appearance. Maybe what he said made some sense, but he was just a little boy, and he hadn't even been to lamplighter school.

The Little Prince kept on pointing out annoying contradictions in their rules.

"You should spend more time obeying the laws rather than picking holes in them" suggested one.

"And you" replied the Prince, "you try so hard to find reasons for not listening to me. All I ask is that you listen to yourselves. Each of you knows what is wrong and what is right…your rules are just silly," he said.

"Prove it!" said one.

"How can I prove it?" replied the Little Prince, "when the proof is that you yourself know what I say is true. You have to be thirsty to enjoy a drink, you have to want to learn something in order to think" quipped the Little Prince before walking away. He knew it was useless talking to lamplighters.

However, many people did listen and thought the Little Prince's teaching was right, even some of the lamplighters put down their lamps and started to listen. But others continued to try and find ways of tricking the Little Prince into saying something wrong so that they could condemn him, but it was very difficult.

BOB PROPHETTE

The Senior Lamplighters were surprised that no-one could win an argument with a child.

"No-one has ever spoken as he does, he seems to have an answer for everything. Even some of the lamplighters are now following him" explained a lamplighter.

"That does not matter" said the Chief Lamplighter, "he's wrong and that's that."

One of the lamplighters, who was more sympathetic to the Little Prince said "I don't see how you can say he is wrong if you don't listen to him and try and understand what he says."

"It's not for us to contradict him, we are the lamplighters. Get him to prove what he says is right, only then will we listen."

And again, the Little Prince was asked to prove he was right.

"Do your lamps illuminate a place already lit?" The Prince asked.

"No" came the reply.

"Just so" said the Little Prince, "no-one can prove the truth. The 'truth' can only be contradicted. If it is contradicted it is not the truth. Your 'truth' is full of contradictions, and of what I have said you can find no fault. Because it is the truth."

"Says you!" said one of the lamplighters.

"And the voice inside you agrees with me, if only you would listen. You have listened too long to other people and have forgotten to listen to the Spirit inside you."

"What is this voice that's supposed to be inside me?" asked one.

"It's the same voice that's in me. You spend all your time discussing what I say, if you did a good deed instead, you would know that I am speaking the truth. Instead, you refuse to do good deeds and spend your time coming up with reasons to justify doing nothing to help others."

"Who taught you to speak like this and say these things?" asked one. "Was it your father?"

"I heard that he doesn't have a father!" jeered another.

"My father is the universe, it made me and is everywhere" affirmed the Little Prince.

"And so you think you are like a god!" exclaimed one.

"You want us to worship you, is that it?" laughed another.

BOB PROPHETTE

"To know what I am talking about, you must do good to other people, as a child does. But you have led your lives not doing good and inventing reasons why you should be able to enjoy your comforts while others are in need. You would rather shut me up than do anything that reduces your comfort. I think you would even have me killed rather than allow me to keep showing you your rules are no good. Rules that do not make you happy and are just a lot of contradictory traditions. Traditions you only follow when it is in your interests to do so. I've told you before and showed you but you neither see nor listen."

"Well at least we have fathers!" jeered one of the lamp-lighters.

"You are a child of the universe, just like me" said the Little Prince. 'I had no father, you are right. You had a father and from your father you learned some things. But if you were born on another planet, and had another father, you would have learned other things. Because you didn't listen to yourselves, you would have believed whatever you were told, so how can you be so convinced you are right?

"I once visited a planet where there were some scientists studying monkeys. They hung bananas at the top of ladders to tempt them to climb. But every time a monkey climbed a ladder, they would soak all the monkeys with a huge hose."

"I think you may be mad!' laughed one of the lamplighters. "Why are you telling us this? It makes no sense."

Some of the lamplighters picked up stones and were about to throw them. But the pilot quickly led the Little Prince away from the angry crowd.

"They call me crazy, but I think it would be easier to make a crazy person understand the truth than them."

"I think you are right" said the pilot as they got safely to the aeroplane and took off.

After they were away and had calmed down a little, the pilot said "I think it will be very hard to convince them. But Little Prince, you didn't finish your story about the scientists and monkeys…"

"Would you like to hear what happened next?" asked the Little Prince.

"Very much" said the pilot.

"Well, after a while the monkeys stopped climbing ladders. Monkeys, as a rule, hate a soaking even more than they love bananas. Then the scientists swapped one of the original monkeys with a new one, who had no idea that he would be soaked if he climbed the ladder. Naturally, seeing the delicious banana, he started to climb. The other monkeys, fearing the hose, grabbed him before he could get very far. They punched, kicked and even bit him to stop him climbing until he gave up. Then the scientists replaced another, and then another of the monkeys, until there were only monkeys who had never had a soaking. The same thing happened each time. Every attempt to climb led to a beating. Eventually none of them ever climbed a ladder, even though they didn't know why."

"Ha!" exclaimed the pilot. "I like that story."

"Most people are like those monkeys" said the Little Prince. "They take seriously words which are of no importance. They are such weak creatures."

"But many people are hearing what you say, leading better lives and helping each other" said the pilot. "I think in the end more people will listen to you than all those lamplighters." He continued, "what you say goes in through people's hearts. What they say goes in by way of the brain and people find reasons to accept or reject what they say. But what you tell people, they already know."

The Little Prince was pleased that his friend understood and nodded in agreement. But the pilot could see he was a

THE GOSPEL ACCORDING TO SAINT X

little disturbed by these last encounters, the lamplighters were getting angrier and angrier.

As they left the planet, the Little Prince sank into a thoughtful silence which lasted a long time.

Chapter Twelve

WHEN THEY WERE ALONE, the Little Prince would sometimes sit quietly and very still. The pilot had learned to leave him to his thoughts at these times, unlikely as he was to be answered, if he had have asked a question.

"What are you thinking about?" asked the pilot after some time.

"I was thinking about my rose" replied the Little Prince. "You know she once got angry with me because I watered the other plants. She would say that she was special and should be treated as such. After all she was so beautiful and took great care of her appearance."

"She wanted a reward for being beautiful?" Asked the pilot.

"Yes" replied the Little Prince. 'She didn't understand that making people happy by being beautiful was a reward in itself."

THE GOSPEL ACCORDING TO SAINT X

"It reminds me" said the pilot, "once when I crashed in a deserted place, I had to get some locals to help me drag the plane to an airfield where I could make repairs. First, I met two people who I told I would give some food to when we arrived at the airfield if they helped me. We made very slow progress, and I was worried we would not reach the airfield before nightfall. So, when I came across some more people, I offered them the same arrangement. Along we went, gathering more people as we made it closer and closer to the airfield at a quicker and quicker pace. Eventually we made it just as the sun set. I made some food for everyone, and we sat down to eat as I thought about the repairs I would make in the morning."

"I'm glad you all made it" said the Little Prince.

"Yes," said the pilot, "but not everyone was happy. Those I had met first seemed to be a little annoyed. When I asked what was wrong, they told me that they had worked longer and should get more food, even though there was enough for everyone."

The Little Prince thought for a moment and then laughed. "The two men you met first thought with their stomachs!"

The pilot laughed along with the Prince as he went on.

BOB PROPHETTE

"If they had thought with their hearts, instead of expecting more food for themselves, they would have been more concerned about whether the last men you met were given enough."

Just then there was a whoosh and to their left they saw a shiny rocket. It came down gently, hardly making a sound as it settled on the sand.

To their surprise the door opened to reveal an astronaut who began waving excitedly at them. He was carrying a purple flag with a single golden star and looked very jolly indeed.

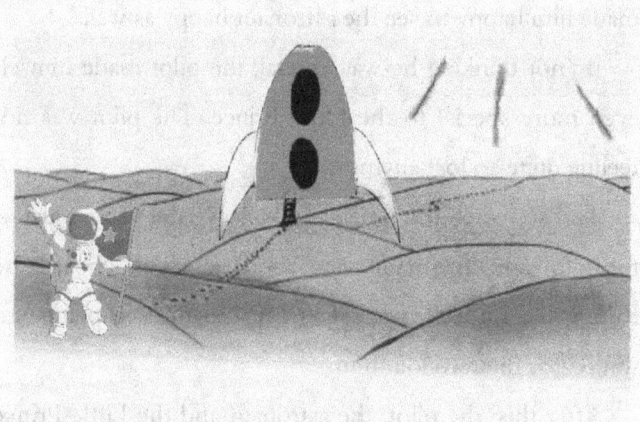

THE GOSPEL ACCORDING TO SAINT X

After he approached them, it became clear that he, like the pilot, was looking for answers and was determined to follow the Prince.

"We can all ride in my rocket" said the astronaut, "there is plenty of room for all of us."

The Little Prince was excited and he looked over to the pilot to see how he would react. They had always travelled together in the aeroplane and he was worried that the pilot would be upset if they travelled in the new rocket.

But the Little Prince needn't have worried. The pilot could see how much the astronaut wanted to be useful. He was very proud of his plane and his piloting skills, but it made him happy to see the astronaut happy as well.

By not thinking he was special, the pilot made himself even more special to the Little Prince. The pilot was not feeling quite so lost anymore.

And so, when the time came to leave the planet, just as the pilot and astronaut were about to climb aboard the rocket, the Little Prince sat as usual in the aeroplane and waited for them to join him.

After this, the pilot, the astronaut and the Little Prince travelled everywhere together, sometimes in the rocket and sometimes in the aeroplane.

BOB PROPHETTE

The astronaut listened attentively to the Little Prince, who gave him his scarf as a present. It can get very cold in space, even for astronauts.

THE GOSPEL ACCORDING TO SAINT X

Chapter Thirteen

THEY TRAVELLED together for some time, visiting lots of new places, meeting new friends and avoiding as many lamplighters as they could. But one day the astronaut was nowhere to be seen.

He had left them as suddenly as he appeared. Full of new ideas the astronaut had decided to set off on his own and see if he could get people to follow him. But no-one did and eventually the astronaut was all alone on a distant planet with only the scarf to keep him warm. His rocket had developed a fault that he was unable to fix.

Feeling very sorry for himself, he asked a fellow traveller to take him to the Little Prince's planet. He was worried that the Little Prince would be angry with him and turn him away. To his surprise the Little Prince welcomed him back with all his heart.

THE GOSPEL ACCORDING TO SAINT X

Even the pilot was pleased to see him, as he could see how happy it made the Little Prince that his little lost astronaut was back. He knew that the Little Prince would always welcome people back, no matter how many times they went away.

In fact if there were 100 astronauts and one went missing, he was sure the Little Prince's thoughts would only be for the one that was lost. Perhaps he had learned that from his time with his sheep.

Chapter Fourteen

THE LAMPLIGHTERS CONTINUED to grow angrier and angrier with the Little Prince. The Senior Lamplighters decided it was time something was done about the odd little man.

"Perhaps he doesn't believe in the power of our lamps" said one of the lamplighters.

"Yes" said another. "Perhaps one lamp isn't enough for him. What about ten lamps? Surely with ten lamps he would have no choice but to obey us?"

And so, a plan was hatched to get ten of the best lamplighters, those with the brightest lamps, to go and wait for the Little Prince on his planet. As soon as he arrived, they were to all turn on their lamps in a show of force, to see if that would get the Prince to obey the rules.

Indeed, when they arrived on the Little Prince's planet and lit their lamps they were a very impressive sight to behold. Thinking that they had solved the problem with the Little Prince, they began to get quite jolly and choreographed a little routine. They spaced themselves out across the Little Prince's planet and made a very pretty, dancing light show while they waited.

They danced and waited and waited and danced, then waited and danced some more. They waited a long time indeed, so long in fact that they started to realise their plan had a flaw.

Plans usually do.

Some of the lamplighters forgot to bring enough batteries! Worried their plan would fail, those without batteries left the Little Prince's planet to get some more. And wouldn't you know it? The Little Prince, the pilot and the astronaut arrived while they were away. In fact, there were only a handful of lamplighters left, and when they turned on their lamps, well, they didn't feel quite as impressive as they had hoped!

The Little Prince could see the lamplighters' disappointment and was sorry for them.

"You know, you should always carry some spare batteries" he said, "as you never know when you might need them."

The Little Prince, the pilot and the astronaut couldn't help but laugh as the lamplighters left without achieving anything much at all.

Turning to the pilot and the astronaut the Little Prince said "well, perhaps the lamplighters are able to teach us something. Dance as much as you like but people should always be prepared. You never know when the dance will stop."

They all smiled.

THE GOSPEL ACCORDING TO SAINT X

Chapter Fifteen

ONE DAY THE ASTRONAUT told his new friends of a planet he had been to that he thought the Little Prince would like. It was a planet where the children taught the adults and the adults learned from the children.

"I would very much like to see this planet," said the Little Prince. "I've been telling people they should be more like children."

And so, as soon as preparations were made, they set off.

I think we may learn something from the people on this planet, thought the Little Prince. In my experience it is always the grown-ups who get things wrong. In fact, thought the Little Prince, if you ask me it's the grown-ups who are to blame for what happens to children. Although he didn't say anything, he looked over at his pilot and his astronaut and smiled. They are like little children with a heavy stone tied around their necks. Where once they were free and happy, now they struggle around with so many cares, not knowing what is wrong or right. They've been told so many conflicting things, their life really is like something very heavy from which they struggle to escape.

Perhaps that's why they fly, he thought. To try and escape from the weight of the world, if only for a short time before they must return. When they are with me flying around, they seem so much happier. As if they've been able to chew through the rope that binds them to their heavy burdens.

And soon the Little Prince, the astronaut and the pilot arrived at the planet. It wasn't exactly how he imagined. Indeed, it was much like other planets. Children still went to school where the adults taught them algebra and geography, just like in so many other places the Little Prince had visited.

But at break times instead of the teachers hiding themselves away in their staff rooms for a rest, they would be joined by many other grown-ups who would come to the school for the special purpose of watching the children play.

Approaching a group of adults who were doing this the Little Prince asked:

"Please, can you tell me what you are doing here?"

"We're waiting to see what happens if a child gets angry" replied one.

"Not many of them do" added another.

"What do they do instead of being angry?" asked the Little Prince.

"It depends" came the reply. "If one child is making the others angry, usually they will not play with him until he stops being naughty. Sometimes a group of children will tell the child who is causing the upset, that they would like him to stop and that usually does the trick, but if it doesn't and the child finds he has no-one to play with, he will usually stop behaving badly quite soon and then re-join the others."

"And is he allowed to re-join, just as before?" asked the Little Prince.

"Oh yes, in fact the child that bears a grudge, who doesn't forgive and welcome the naughty child back, is then considered the naughty one and it's him that gets excluded from the play. As long as the first child is truly sorry of course."

"But children rarely get angry, they are quick to say sorry and quick to forgive" explained one of the observers.

"Why do you think that is?" asked the Little Prince.

"Children want, above anything else, to play and have fun. Being angry just gets in the way. Being kind and welcoming means you can play for longer and in more interesting ways" said another of the observers.

"You can't very well have fun if you are angry" said the Little Prince.

"Exactly!" said one, who appeared to be a teacher. "On this planet we teach children some things, and they teach us others. They don't know a lot about mathematics, but they know how to have fun!"

"And do you have lamplighters here?" asked the pilot.

"Lamplighters? asked one with a puzzled expression.

"Yes, they say they know what's wrong and what's right and use their lamps to tell people so" said the pilot.

"No, we don't have any of those" was the reply.

"And what about people who count up wrong-doings and tell you how much you have to pay?" asked the pilot.

"No, none of those either. We learn from the children what is wrong and what is right. Or rather they remind us of what we already know" said a different observer.

"What else have you learned from the children?" asked the Prince.

BOB PROPHETTE

"Well, let's see. Commitment is another thing. People should be responsible for the things they love. Once you love something and that thing loves you, you shouldn't stop. Ever."

"And how does that work?" asked the pilot who had always struggled with friendship.

"Well for children, friendship is forever. You don't just stop being friends with someone because it's not convenient anymore or because you are not having as much fun as you used to. Children don't do it because they know it's like a virus."

"A virus?" asked the pilot.

"If one child is rejected, he becomes unhappy, he makes another child unhappy, and so on and so on. The unhappiness spreads…like a virus. Pretty soon that unhappiness comes back around, usually before the end of playtime. And so, you don't see much of that kind of behaviour."

It's like tending to baobab seeds, thought the Little Prince. But he wasn't sure these people knew what baobab seeds were, so he kept that to himself.

"It's a bit like in the Air Force' said the pilot. 'You swear allegiance to your fellow pilots. You promise to look after one another, no-one gets left behind."

"Ah, but this is different to a promise" said one. "They just do it."

'Air Force?" asked one of the observers.

The pilot suddenly realised that if no one got angry for long on this planet they were unlikely to have an Air Force. But he decided to explain anyway.

"Where I come from, we have an Air Force in case we are attacked by the people of another country."

"People of another country?" questioned one. "But isn't everyone alike?"

"Yes, they are alike, but they're foreign at the same time, they behave differently, dress differently and so on" explained the pilot.

"We learned from children that it really makes no sense to treat people differently. You can't play with someone you don't treat the same as everyone else. Not for long anyway."

Others in the group were keen to hear more about the pilot's planet.

"Who pays for the Air Force?" asked one.

The pilot went on to explain that the government collected taxes and promised to use the money to defend everyone if they were attacked. The people promised to pay the taxes if they did so.

"Do you have to pay the taxes?" asked one.

"Yes, you do, otherwise there would be trouble" said the pilot.

"It sounds very complicated. Wouldn't it be easier if you didn't get angry and treated everyone alike? Then there would be more time for fun" asked one.

"And what if the pilots don't want to fight?" asked another.

"They have to, that's all part of the arrangement" replied the pilot.

"And if they don't?"

"They would be court marshalled and put in a prison."

"Is the prison paid for with taxes?" another asked.

The pilot replied yes, but by now no-one was listening to him anymore. The observers had returned to watching the children. It was so much more interesting than what the pilot was saying.

The pilot continued talking if only to himself and as he did, he noticed a child had come over and was sitting at his feet.

"Hello!" said the child.

"Hello!" replied the pilot.

"Why are you talking to yourself?" asked the child.

'I think my friends think that I'm talking nonsense" said the pilot. "Where I come from it is very different to here."

"That sounds like a great game" said the child. "Let's take turns saying nonsense things to each other."

"Okay" agreed the pilot.

Soon, the others saw what the child and the pilot were doing and joined in the game. They took turns in saying something nonsensical until they had a new story that was so crazy it made everyone laugh to think about it.

The Little Prince liked the game best of all as he was very good at saying things that made little sense to people.

But after a while, they stopped the game, and the Prince looked a little worried.

"You know" he said "I am afraid that next time we meet some lamplighters there is going to be trouble."

"Why don't we just stay here?" said the pilot.

"But I like travelling around, I'm not ready to stop. Besides if we stop now, it'll be like letting the lamplighters win."

"But what if they try to hurt you?" asked the pilot.

"I'm not worried about that" said the Little Prince. "I don't worry about my body too much, it's more important to live the way you believe is right. It's wrong to live another way, just because others think you should. The most important thing is to love. If it's a choice between living in fear and living courageously so you can love, then it's not really a choice you'd have to think for a long time about. Besides, someone must stand up to these lamplighters. If no-one stands up to them, then nothing can change. Almost anything can be made better, unless you are confused about what 'better' is. Then nothing at all can be made better, no matter how you try. These lamplighters are confusing people. That needs to stop. It's the most important thing I can think of."

"I don't think this is going to be easy" said the pilot, "there are an awful lot of lamplighters. They like their lamps and they like their temples. They're unlikely to give them up easily."

"No, it won't be easy" agreed the Little Prince. "I expect before things get better, they may even get worse."

Suddenly, the Little Prince went very pale. A terrible thought had just come into his mind. For a moment he saw a lamplighter telling others what they should and shouldn't do, but making them think it was the Little Prince's teaching. That made his whole body shudder. That would be very bad indeed thought the Little Prince, very bad indeed.

THE GOSPEL ACCORDING TO SAINT X

Chapter Sixteen

AS TIME WENT ON, more and more people started to agree with what the Little Prince was saying. This continued to annoy the lamplighters. In fact, they decided something really had to be done and so they gathered in the temple and began to consider what they could do.

They agreed that if things went on like this, they would end up in a situation where no one anywhere would listen to them any longer. Many ideas were discussed but no one seemed able to agree.

Then, the Chief Lamplighter stood up and announced "It is clear that the Little Prince must die."

Many of those present looked confused.

"Isn't it written in our laws that people should not kill each other?"

"This is true,' confirmed the Chief Lamplighter, "but I've been thinking, sometimes it is necessary to kill one in order to save many. So that is what we must do."

There was much chattering and many looks were exchanged but eventually all were agreed.

"But how do we get him to come to somewhere we can grab him?" asked one.

"We'll throw a party and send him an invitation. If he likes parties, he is sure to come" said another.

When the invitation arrived both the pilot and the astronaut thought it was a very bad idea for the Little Prince to go.

But the Little Prince had begun to see that this was the only way. He hadn't been sure what his body was for, maybe it was for this.

When they arrived near the place where the party was planned many people came out to greet the Little Prince. He was very pleased to receive such a greeting. One man came with a beautiful horse and asked if the Little Prince would like to ride on it the rest of the way.

'But if I ride on the horse, what will you ride?' asked the Little Prince.

BOB PROPHETTE

The man pointed to a small donkey, who looked very young. To the man's surprise the Little Prince handed him back the reins to the horse and instead got up on the donkey. And that is how he set off for the party. It made the Little Prince chuckle to be arriving in such a way.

But first the Little Prince decided to go once more to the temple and again set free all the animals. Then he sat on the steps and began to tell more of his stories and answer questions, but now his words seemed to have more urgency.

And the Little Prince was very pleased to hear the way these people talked. They really had started to think for themselves. And so, he was less worried about what would happen after he had gone.

But he knew he was in danger if he stayed too long at the temple, and he wasn't quite ready to meet the lamplighters just yet.

The lamplighters had heard that the Little Prince had arrived but were annoyed that they could not find him.

"He seems to be hiding from us" said one of them.

"Then offer a reward to anyone who will lead us to him" said the Chief Lamplighter.

And so, notices were put up all around the town, but for a long time, no-one came to claim the reward.

WANTED!

Have you seen the one who calls himself the Little Prince?

-REWARD-

Then, after many hours, one appeared. It was the astronaut.

"I can help you if you want to find the Little Prince" he said somewhat nervously. "I have come to claim the reward but you must not hurt him."

The Chief Lamplighter promised it would be so, unconcerned about adding a lie to a murder for the sake of 'his' people.

BOB PROPHETTE

Later the astronaut joined the Little Prince and the pilot who were sitting down to eat. The Little Prince knew that the astronaut had been to see the lamplighters but he didn't say anything. Instead, they enjoyed a last meal together. The Little Prince knew it was time.

When they had eaten, the Little Prince told them what would happen next.

"Tomorrow," he said, "the lamplighters will come and they will take me. I will have to go away. These lamplighters seem to want to do me harm and I have decided to let them. I will not fight back. People will see just how wrong the lamplighters are. It will be an example to them for the future."

He continued "for some time, I have been afraid that the lamplighters would come, they would threaten my life and I would fight them and become like them. But that's not how it will happen."

The pilot said that if the lamplighters tried to hurt him and the Little Prince did not fight back, he would.

And the Little Prince said that he wanted to go outside so that he could be alone and think. He remembered back to a long time ago after he met the fox and went into the desert. The echo had challenged him to live without his body, if the Spirit was more important to him than the flesh. He had thought how wonderful that would be, but now the time had come when his body was in serious danger. He found himself a little scared.

The pilot too was becoming more and more upset at the idea that he would soon be losing his friend.

Seeing the pilot upset made the Little Prince feel even worse. He would miss his friend and knew his friend would miss him, but he tried to put on a cheerful face.

"Don't worry" he said. "A good thing is about to happen, though it might not seem like that for a while. I am tired of this body and have no more use for it anyway. It's become too heavy for me."

Chapter Seventeen

THE PILOT, THE LITTLE PRINCE and the astronaut all went to bed. But while the Little Prince and the astronaut slept soundly under the stars, the pilot was restless.

He wanted to ask the Little Prince many more questions but was afraid to wake him. Anyway, he thought, if that little man has taught me anything it's that I have to listen to myself. And so, the pilot began to go over in his head all that he had seen the Little Prince say and do.

The pilot kept returning to the same thing. The Little Prince wanted people to love one another and there is no greater love than to sacrifice one's life for others.

Is that what tomorrow will bring? thought the pilot.

He will set the ultimate example by allowing the lamplighters to kill him and not fight back.

His death will be his final message about how to live well.

He will die so that everyone can see the truth, what is false and how to make good decisions and lead a good life.

THE GOSPEL ACCORDING TO SAINT X

When people are confused, they can think about his example. They can think about how much he taught people and how he suffered for it.

They will see how it is the lamplighters that cause suffering and be able to recognise those people more easily.

His message will go on forever and in that sense his Spirit will never die.

The pilot began to cry and as he sobbed he finally fell fast asleep.

Chapter Eighteen

IN THE MORNING they were surrounded by lamplighters and guards. Some guards approached the Little Prince with mean looks on their faces. The pilot quickly stood and placed himself between the guards and the Little Prince.

But the Little Prince told the pilot to stop. "This is the way it must be."

Turning to the lamplighters he said "you needn't have sent any guards, I would have come willingly; I'm not hiding from you."

The guards took the Little Prince to the temple and stood him before the Chief Lamplighter.

The pilot had followed the Little Prince and was standing outside. Some of the lamplighters recognised him.

"You are the friend of the Little Prince" said one.

The pilot was afraid.

"No, no, no" said the pilot, "you are confused. I promise I'm not a friend of his."

"But we saw you with him, you and that astronaut" they said.

The pilot hurried away and was very sad.

How hard it is to follow the Little Prince's example, he thought. I know he is right, I feel it, and yet how quickly I have become angry, denied our friendship and lied to save my skin. How wretched am I? Three times weak. I must try harder to be like the Little Prince.

Inside the temple, the Chief Lamplighter began his questioning.

"So, you think your rules are better than ours?" he began.

"I think your rules are stupid" replied the Prince.

One of the guards slapped the Little Prince across his face.

"I have shown you how silly your rules are. If your rules are better, tell me what is wrong with my teaching" said the Little Prince, rubbing his cheek.

"You want to destroy our temple?" asked the Chief Lamplighter.

"No. I said your temple was a waste of bricks" replied the Prince.

BOB PROPHETTE

"You think you are a god!" went on the Chief Lamplighter.

"No. I said God is the Spirit inside of me."

"Blasphemy!" cried several of the lamplighters.

"You are condemned to death!" said the Chief Lamplighter banging his lamp pole on the ground.

"Take him to the King, to pass sentence."

And so, the Little Prince was marched out of the temple and all the way to the palace of the King.

When they arrived the King looked somewhat bewildered. He sat on a chair that was at the same time simple and majestic. Seeing the angry looks on the faces of the guards and lamplighters he turned to the Little Prince.

"Ah!" he said. "A subject. How do you do?"

"Good eve…" started the Little Prince courteously, before he was cut off.

"This is the Little Prince. He has broken all our rules and said many things he shouldn't."

"I see" said the King. "But you have your own punishments for those who break your rules, how much does he have to pay?"

"We don't want him to pay a fine" said the Chief Lamplighter. "We want him executed."

"Executed!" exclaimed the King. "I don't think I can do that, can I? Not according to *my* science of government."

"Only a King can order someone to be executed" replied the lamplighter. "Do it now and we'll have the guards carry out your order."

"But I don't want to order anyone to be killed. That is a very bad thing. He seems such a nice little man. What has he done that is so wrong?" asked the King.

"He has told people that they should not follow our rules. He even made up his own rules. The people think that he is their ruler."

"But aren't I their ruler?" asked the King hesitantly. "I do like to be obeyed."

Turning to the Little Prince, he asked "Is it true, little man? Do you think you are the ruler? Because if you do, we might have a problem."

"Everyone who listens to what I say and does what I do, does not need a ruler. They can become their own rulers. They can be Kings themselves."

"What a funny little man you are" chuckled the King. "How can everyone be a King? That's my job. My authority must be respected. I don't like insubordination."

After a pause the King went on.

"I won't enjoy it, but I think maybe you will have to be executed after all."

He fumbled with his robes, then continued, "but today is my birthday and I don't want to execute anyone on my birthday, so if you say you are sorry, and you truly, truly mean it, I will let you off."

The Little Prince remained silent.

"No!" Shouted the lamplighters. "He must be executed. If he is not executed, there will be lots of trouble."

"Trouble?" asked the King, confused.

"Yes" said the lamplighter. "What the Little Prince is telling the people changes them. They are thinking new thoughts. They are not listening to us. There is bound to be trouble."

When he heard this, the King understood that, reluctant as he was to harm anyone, he probably had no choice.

"Oh. Very well! I don't like trouble." He fell silent. His lips seemed frozen by the sense of something irreparable. After a long pause he said "Very well. Soldiers! Take him to the mountain and push him off. It's not my fault. We can't have any trouble. I won't be able to rule."

And so, the Little Prince was led to the top of a very high mountain. As they climbed up the soldiers made him very uncomfortable, pushing and shoving, poking him with their lamps.

The Little Prince remained calm.

The pilot watched from a far. He was very, very sad. He wanted to stop what was happening, but he knew this was what his friend wanted.

BOB PROPHETTE

When they had reached the summit, the Little Prince said "I forgive you for what you are doing to me."

The soldiers moved forward so that the Little Prince was pushed right to the edge. Looking down at the jagged rocks below. the Little Prince said "Oh dear" quietly to himself.

"Please, may I have a drink of water?"

He began to think over all that had happened on his journey. Of his friend the fox who spoke the truth that few could hear. Of the mountain's echo that questioned what he knew. Of the librarian and his books. A library that contained the truth that no one read or could understand. Of the lamplighters and their jolly lamps that they used without thinking. Of the tax collector and his friends who could only think in circles. Of the temple official and his unending task. The thirsty men in their dry place. Of the perfume that tickled his feet. Of those that heard and talked but couldn't do or act. Of his little astronaut. His dear little astronaut. How none of them seemed to have the understanding of a child. And his friend the pilot who had learned so much and in whom there was hope.

Then one of the soldiers gave him a cup. He drank the water, returned the cup, closed his eyes, felt a shove and felt himself begin to fall.

THE GOSPEL ACCORDING TO SAINT X

But before he reached the jagged rocks below, who should appear but the pilot in his airplane.

The pilot carefully flew and matched his speed to that of his falling friend. Miraculously he caught him. The Little Prince landed on top of the plane with a heavy thump, his arms stretched out across the aeroplane's wings as if on a cross...

BOB PROPHETTE

The soldiers watched as the Little Prince's body was flown far, far away.

The End.

THE GOSPEL ACCORDING TO SAINT X

Epilogue

Did the Little Prince survive dear reader?

It's hard to tell.

His fall was very far and the thud of his body as he hit the plane very loud. But his friend was a very capable pilot and had learned just how to catch a falling prince.

*****

The reader will I hope forgive the uncertainty introduced by this ending to the re-telling of the Gospels. It is an ambiguity that reflects both the story of the Gospels and also the story of the Little Prince.

In *The Little Prince*, the ambiguity is present since although the events and the demeanours of the characters leading up to the Little Prince's departure clearly suggest a physical death, no body is found. Similarly, although not part of Tolstoy's re-telling, the disappearance of Christ's body from the tomb and his subsequent re-appearance to several disciples, leaves room for hope and doubt.

It is also an ambiguity present in the concern expressed by the pilot, who, realising that he had left the planned sheep's muzzle undrawn becomes concerned that it will eat more than the baobab shoots. Just as it is present in Christ's chilling final cry:

Eli, Eli Lama Sabachthani?!

(My God, my God! Why hast thou forsaken me?).

Your author believes both the Gospels and *The Little Prince* are invitations to faith and illustrations of the rewards that faith in the immaterial offers us.

So next time you see what looks like a hat, look again. It *might* not be as it first appears. But then again, it might. It's the uncertainty that makes life so very interesting, so hopeful.

I'm not sure the experience of writing this book has led to my Metanoia. I like to think it has. Friends think I'm a Christian. I'm not. Unless Christian means 'question everything, question why you are questioning, then do what you think is right'. If you read this, or have a similar experience, please be good enough to write to me at once, it will be a great comfort.

BOB PROPHETTE

Appendix: Terminology/Interpretation

The references to 'The Father' in Tolstoy's gospels remain, I fear, a little confusing to modern readers, having connotations of a physical thing. I think the term is perhaps better thought of as 'the source of life', the 'ultimate parent'. Following the discovery of DNA, the code of life, I think we have a new way of appreciating this idea. Hence phrases in Tolstoy's Gospel's such as 'The Father's will' may be better read as 'our innate purpose'. I'm not crediting Jesus with an understanding of biological evolution. That would be absurd. But its social equivalent, cultural evolution, would not have been a mystery. Jesus's words show that he is very aware that people could grow spiritually, and through example help others to do the same. Overtime such adaptations would be carried on as people followed good examples set by their parents and those around them.

Similarly, references to the 'Kingdom of God' may confuse and I have equated it to the idea of Peace/Happiness, in that when someone has found peace, with themselves and with others, they can be said to have reached a kind of heaven. Also, many commentators have made clear that the idea of an external heaven is not found in the Gospels and is an invention of those who came after Jesus.

'Eternal life' is a trickier concept but I have used the idea that this is about 'species level' survival in eternity. Personally, I find it hard to believe that Jesus or Tolstoy meant individual immortality when they spoke about eternal life. Such a concept seems irrevocably selfish. To me the whole idea of 'resurrection' is a fantasy invented by the early

THE GOSPEL ACCORDING TO SAINT X

church to make their nascent religion palatable to the pagan masses. It is telling that Tolstoy's Gospels end with Christ's death. Rather, the eternal life is the life of the Spirit. A life that goes on in the universe if we refrain from destroying ourselves. Becoming extinct. That would be a shame. But then, as the Little Prince said "You never can tell!"

Miracles. I have included only one 'miracle' in the text, as Tolstoy did, but as you can see, it's psychology, not the supernatural, that holds the power. Christ could not cure people any more than a snake oil purveyor could. But people are often deluded and just need someone to tell them what is what. Or they just need a little loving kindness.

The commandments and the Lord's Prayer. This was the most difficult part of the text to write by far. I think this is the area Tolstoy had most difficulty with as well. I have done my best to interpret the true meaning of what Jesus is supposed to have said, as relayed by Tolstoy. I'm not satisfied I have fully understood or captured it properly. As such this is something I think about often and perhaps that's the point.

BOB PROPHETTE

The Little Prince – A Summary[1]

The narrator begins with a discussion on the nature of grownups and their inability to perceive 'important things'. As a test to determine if a grownup is as enlightened as a child, he shows them a picture depicting a boa constrictor that has eaten an elephant. The grownups always reply that the picture depicts a hat, and so he knows to only talk of "reasonable" things to them, rather than the fanciful.

The narrator becomes an aircraft pilot, and one day, his plane crashes in the Sahara desert, far from civilisation. The narrator has an eight-day supply of water and must fix his airplane. Here, he is greeted unexpectedly by a young boy nicknamed "The Little Prince." The Prince has golden hair, a loveable laugh and will repeat questions until they are answered.

The Prince asks the narrator to draw a sheep. The narrator first shows him the picture of the elephant inside the snake, which, to the narrator's surprise, the Prince interprets correctly. After three failed attempts at drawing a sheep, the frustrated narrator draws a simple crate, claiming that the sheep is inside. The Prince exclaims that this was exactly the drawing he wanted.

Over the course of eight days in the desert, while the narrator attempts to repair his plane, the Prince recounts his

---

[1] Extracted unaltered from Wikipedia, 4/11/2023.

life story. He begins describing his tiny home planet: in effect, a house-sized asteroid known as 'B 612' on Earth. The asteroid's most prominent features are three minuscule volcanoes (two active and one dormant or extinct) and a variety of plants.

The Prince describes his earlier days cleaning the volcanoes and weeding unwanted seeds and sprigs that infest his planet's soil; in particular, pulling out baobab trees that are constantly on the verge of overrunning the surface. If the baobabs are not rooted out the moment they are recognised, their roots can have a catastrophic effect on the tiny planet. Therefore, the Prince wants a sheep to eat the undesirable plants, but worries it will also eat plants with thorns.

The Prince tells of his love for a vain and silly rose that began growing on the asteroid's surface some time ago. The rose is given to pretension, exaggerating ailments to gain attention and have the Prince care for her. The Prince says he nourished the rose and tended to her, making a screen and glass globe to protect her from the cold and wind, watering her and keeping the caterpillars off.

Although the Prince fell in love with the rose, he also began to feel that she was taking advantage of him, and he resolved to leave the planet to explore the rest of the universe. Upon their goodbyes, the rose apologises for failing to show that she loved him. She wishes him well and turns down his desire to leave her in the glass globe, saying she will protect herself. The Prince laments that he did not understand how to love his rose while he was with her and should have listened to her kind actions, rather than her vain words.

The Prince has since visited six other planets, each of which was inhabited by a single, irrational, narrow-minded adult, each meant to critique an element of society. They include:

- A King with no subjects, who only issues orders that will be followed, such as commanding the sun to set at sunset.
- A conceited man who only wants the praise which comes from admiration and being the most admirable person on his otherwise uninhabited planet.
- A drunkard who drinks to forget the shame of drinking.
- A businessman who is blind to the beauty of the stars and instead endlessly counts and catalogues them in order to "own" them all (critiquing materialism).
- A lamplighter on a planet so small that a full day lasts a minute. He wastes his life blindly following orders to extinguish and relight the lamppost every 30 seconds to correspond with his planet's day and night.
- An elderly geographer who has never been anywhere, or seen any of the things he records, providing a caricature of specialisation in the contemporary world.

It is the geographer who tells the Prince that his rose is an ephemeral being, which is not recorded. He recommends that the Prince next visit the planet Earth. The visit to Earth begins with a deeply pessimistic appraisal of humanity. The six absurd people the Prince encounters earlier comprise, according to the narrator, just about the entire adult world. On earth there were:

111 kings, 7,000 geographers, 900,000 businessmen, 7,500,000 tipplers, 311,000,000 conceited men. That is to say, about 2,000,000,000 grown-ups.

Since the Prince landed in a desert, he believed that Earth was uninhabited. He then met a yellow snake that claimed to have the power to return him to his home, if he ever wished to return. The Prince next met a desert flower, who told him that she had only seen a handful of men in this part of the world and that they had no roots, letting the wind blow them around and living hard lives. After climbing the highest mountain he had ever seen, the Prince hoped to see the whole of Earth, thus finding the people. However he saw only the enormous, desolate landscape. When the Prince called out, his echo answered him, which he interpreted as the voice of a boring person who only repeats what another says.

The Prince encounters a whole row of rosebushes, becoming downcast at having once thought that his own rose was unique and thinking his rose had lied about being unique. He began to feel that he was not a great prince at all, as his planet contained only three tiny volcanoes and a flower that he now thought of as common. He laid down on the grass and wept, until a fox came along.

The fox desired to be tamed and taught the Prince how to tame him. By being tamed, something goes from being ordinary and just like all the others to being special and unique. There are drawbacks since the connection can lead to sadness and longing when apart.

From the fox, the Prince learns that his rose was indeed unique and special because she was the object of the Prince's love and time. He had 'tamed' her and now she was more precious than all of the roses he had seen in the garden. Upon their sad departing, the fox imparts a secret: important things can only be seen with the heart, not the eyes.

The Prince finally met two people from Earth:

- A railway switchman who told him how passengers constantly rushed from one place to another aboard trains, never satisfied with where they were and not knowing what they were after; only the children among them ever bothered to look out the windows.

- A merchant who talked to the Prince about his product, a pill that eliminated the need to drink for a week, saving people 53 minutes.

BOB PROPHETTE

Back in the present moment, it is the eighth day after the narrator's plane crash and the narrator and the Prince are dying of thirst. The Prince has become visibly morose and saddened over his recollections and longs to return home and see his flower.

The Prince finds a well, thus saving them. The narrator later finds the Prince talking to the snake, discussing his return home and his desire to see his rose again, who, he worries, has been left to fend for herself. The Prince bids an emotional farewell to the narrator and states that if it looks as though he has died, it is only because his body was too heavy to take with him to his planet. The Prince warns the narrator not to watch him leave, as it will upset him. The narrator, realising what will happen, refuses to leave the Prince's side. The Prince consoles the narrator by saying that he only need look at the stars to think of the Prince's loveable laughter, and that it will seem as if all the stars are laughing. The Prince then walks away from the narrator and allows the snake to bite him, soundlessly falling down.

The next morning, the narrator is unable to find the Prince's body. He finally manages to repair his airplane and leave the desert. It is left up to the reader to determine if the Prince returned home or died. The story ends with a drawing of the landscape where the Prince and the narrator met and where the snake took the Prince's corporeal life. The narrator requests to be immediately contacted by anyone in that area encountering a small person with golden curls who refuses to answer any questions.

THE GOSPEL ACCORDING TO SAINT X

Tolstoy's Gospels in Brief – A Summary of the Chapters

JESUS in his childhood spoke of God as his Father. There was in Judaea at that time a prophet named John, who preached the coming of God on earth. He said that if people changed their way of life, considered all men equal, and instead of injuring, helped one another, God would appear and His Kingdom would be established on earth.

HAVING heard this preaching, Jesus withdrew into the desert to consider the meaning of man's life and his relation to the infinite origin of all, called God. Jesus recognized as his Father that infinite source of being whom John called God.

Having stayed in the desert for some days without food, Jesus suffered hunger and thought within himself.

As a son of God Almighty I ought to be all-powerful as He is, but now that I want to eat and cannot create bread to satisfy my hunger, I see that I am not all-powerful. But to this reflection he made answer: I cannot make bread out of stones, but I can refrain from eating, and so, though I am not all-powerful in the body I am all-powerful in spirit and can quell the body. Therefore I am a son of God not through the flesh but through the spirit.

Then he said to himself: I am a son of the spirit. Let me therefore renounce the body and do away with it. But to this

THE GOSPEL ACCORDING TO SAINT X

he replied: I am born as spirit embodied in flesh. Such is the will of my Father and I must not resist His will.

But-he went on thinking-if I can neither satisfy the needs of my body nor free myself from it, then I ought to devote myself to the body and enjoy all the pleasures it can afford me. But to this he replied: I cannot satisfy the needs of my body, and cannot rid myself of it; but my life is all-powerful in that it is the spirit of my Father. Therefore in my body I should serve the spirit, my Father, and work for Him alone.

And becoming convinced that man's true life lies only in the spirit of the Father, Jesus left the desert and began to declare this teaching to men. He said that the spirit dwelt in him, that henceforth the heavens were open and the powers of heaven brought to man, and a free and boundless life had begun for man, and that all men, however unfortunate in the body, might be happy.

THE Jews who considered themselves Orthodox worshipped an external God, whom they regarded as creator and ruler of the universe. According to their teaching this external God had made an agreement with them by which He had promised to help them if they would worship Him. A chief condition of this alliance was the keeping of Saturday, the Sabbath.

But Jesus said: The Sabbath is a human institution. That man should live in the spirit is more than all external ceremonies. Like all external forms of religion the keeping of the Sabbath involves a delusion. You are forbidden to do anything on the Sabbath, but good actions should always be done and if keeping the Sabbath hinders the doing of a good action then the keeping of the Sabbath is an error.

According to the Orthodox Jews another condition of the agreement with God was avoidance of intercourse with unbelievers.

BOB PROPHETTE

Of this Jesus said that God desires not sacrifice to Himself, but that men should love one another.

Yet another condition of the agreement related to rules for washing and purifying, as to which Jesus said that what God demands is not external cleanliness, but pity and love towards man. He also said that external rules are harmful, and that the church tradition is itself an evil. Their church tradition set aside the most important things, such as love for one's mother and father-and justified this by its traditional railings.

Of all the external regulations of the old law defining the cases in which a man was considered to have defiled himself, Jesus said: Know all of you, that nothing from outside can defile a man, only what he thinks and does can defile him.

After this Jesus went to Jerusalem, the city considered holy, and entered into the temple where the Orthodox considered that God Himself dwelt, arid there he said that it was useless to offer God sacrifices, that man is more important than a temple, and that our only duty is to love our neighbor and help him.

Furthermore Jesus taught that it is not necessary to worship God in any particular place, but to serve the Father in spirit and in deed. The spirit cannot be seen or shown. The spirit is man's consciousness of his sonship to the Infinite Spirit. No temple is necessary. The true temple is the society of men united in love. He said that all external worship of God is not only false and injurious when it conduces to wrong-doing-like the Jew's worship which prescribed killing as a punishment-and allowed the neglect of parents-but also because a man performing external rites accounts himself righteous and free from the need of doing what love demands. He said that only he seeks what is good and does good deeds, who feels his own imperfections. To do good deeds a man must be conscious of his own faults, but external worship leads to a false self-satisfaction. All external worship is unnecessary, and should be thrown aside. Deeds of love are incompatible with ceremonial performances, and good cannot be done in that way. Man is a spiritual son of God and should therefore serve the Father in spirit.

JOHN'S pupils asked Jesus what he meant by his 'kingdom of heaven' and he answered them: The heaven I preach is the same as that preached by John-that all men, however poor, may be happy.

And Jesus said to the people: John is the first prophet to preach to men a Kingdom of God which is not of the external world, but in the soul of man. The Orthodox went to hear John, but understood nothing because they know only what they have themselves invented about an external God; they teach their inventions and are astonished that no one pays heed to them. But John preached the truth of the Kingdom of God within us, and therefore he did more than anybody before him. By his teaching the law and the prophets, and all external forms of worship, are superseded. Since he taught, it has been made clear that the Kingdom of God is in man's soul.

The beginning and the end of everything is the soul of man. Every man, though he realizes that he was conceived by a bodily father in his mother's womb, is conscious also that he has within him a spirit that is free, intelligent, and independent of the body.

That eternal spirit proceeding from the infinite, is the origin of all and is what we call God. We know Him only as we recognize Him within ourselves. That spirit is the source of our life; we must rank it above everything and by it we must live. By making it the basis of our life we obtain true and everlasting life. The Father-spirit who has given that spirit to man cannot have sent it to deceive men-that while conscious of everlasting life in themselves they should lose it. This infinite spirit in man must have been given that through him men should have an infinite life. Therefore the man who conceives of this spirit as his life has infinite life, while a man who does not so conceive it has no true life. Men can themselves choose life or death: life in the spirit, or death in the flesh. The life of the spirit is goodness and light: the life of the flesh is evil and darkness. To believe in the spirit. means to do good deeds; to disbelieve means to do evil. Goodness is life, evil is death. God-an external creator, the beginning of all beginnings-we do not know. Our conception of Him can only be this: that He has sown the spirit in men as a sower sows his seed, everywhere, not discriminating as to what part of the field; and the seed that falls on good ground grows, but what falls on sterile ground perishes. The spirit alone gives life to men, and it depends on them to preserve it or lose it. For the spirit, evil does not exist. Evil is an illusion of life. There is only that which lives and that which does not live.

Thus the world presents itself to all men, and each man has a consciousness of the kingdom of heaven in his soul. Each one can of his own free will enter that kingdom or not. To enter it he must believe in the life of the spirit, for he who believes in that life has everlasting life.

JESUS was sorry for people because they did not know true happiness, therefore he taught them. He said: Blessed are they who have no property or fame and do not care for them, and unhappy are they who seek riches and fame; for the destitute and the oppressed are in the Father's will, but the rich and famous seek only rewards from men in this temporal life.

To fulfil the will of the Father do not fear to be poor and despised, but rejoice that you can show men what true happiness is.

THE GOSPEL ACCORDING TO SAINT X

To carry out the will of the Father which gives life and welfare to all men, five commandments must be obeyed:

The first commandment is to do no ill to anyone so as not to arouse anger, for evil begets evil.

The second commandment is not to go after women and not to desert the wife with whom you have once been joined; for desertion and change of wives causes all the world's dissoluteness.

The third commandment is to take no oath of any kind. A man can promise nothing, for he is altogether in the Father's power; and oaths are taken for bad purposes.

The fourth commandment is not to resist evil, not to condemn, and not to go to law; but to endure wrong and to do even more than people demand, for every man is full of faults and incapable of guiding others. By taking revenge, we only teach others to do the same.

The fifth commandment is not to discriminate between fellow-countrymen and foreigners, for all are children of one Father.

These five commandments should be observed not to win praise from men, but for your own welfare; therefore do not pray, or fast, in the sight of men.

The Father knows all that people need, and there is no need to pray for anything; all that is necessary is to seek to be in the Father's will. And His will is that we should not feel enmity towards anyone. It is unnecessary to fast, for men fast merely to win praise from men and their praise should be avoided. It is necessary only to take care to live in the Father's will, and the rest will all be added of itself. A man concerned with the things of the body cannot be concerned with the kingdom of heaven. Even though a man does not trouble about food and clothing, he can live: the Father will give life. All that is needful is to be in the will of the Father at the present moment, for the Father gives his children what they need. Desire only the power of the spirit, which the Father gives. The five commandments show the path to the kingdom of heaven, and this narrow path alone leads to everlasting life.

False teachers-wolves pretending to be sheep always try to lead people astray from this path. Beware of them! False teachers can always be detected by the fact that they teach evil in the name of good. If they teach violence and executions they are false teachers. By what they teach they may be known.

Not he fulfills the Father's will who calls on the name of God, but he who does what is good. He who fulfills these five commandments will have a secure and true life, of which nothing can deprive him: but he who does not fulfil them will have an insecure life which will soon be taken from him, leaving him nothing.

The teaching of Jesus surprised and attracted the people by the fact that it recognized all men as free. It was the fulfilment of Isaiah's prophecy, that God's chosen one would bring light to men, would overcome evil and re-establish truth, not by violence but by gentleness, meekness, and kindness.

WISDOM lies in recognizing life as the offspring of the Father s spirit. People set themselves the aims of the bodily life, and in seeking these aims torment themselves and others. But they will find full satisfaction in the life meant for them-the life of the spirit-if they accept the doctrine of the spiritual life and of subduing and controlling the body.

It happened once that Jesus asked a woman of another religion to give him some water to drink. She refused on the plea that she was of a different faith. Jesus then said to her: If you understood that he who is asking for water is a living man in whom the spirit of the Father lives, you would not refuse him, but by doing a kindness would try to unite yourself in spirit with the Father, and that spirit would give you not such water as this-after drinking which a man thirsts again-but water that gives everlasting life. One need not pray to God in any special place, but should serve Him, by deeds of love-by ministering to those in whom His spirit dwells.

And Jesus said to his pupils: The true food of man is to fulfil the will of the Fatherspirit, and this fulfilment is always possible. Our whole life is a gathering up of the fruits of the spirit sown within us by the Father. Those fruits are the good we do to men. We should do good to men unceasingly and expect no reward.

After this Jesus happened to be in Jerusalem and came to a bathing-place beside which lay a sick man, waiting for a miracle to cure him. Jesus said this to him: Do not expect to be cured by a miracle, but live according to your strength and do not mistake the meaning of life. The invalid obeyed Jesus, got up, and went away. Seeing this, the Orthodox began to reproach Jesus for having cured an invalid on the Sabbath. Jesus said to them: I have done nothing new. I have only done what our common Father-spirit does. He lives and gives life to men, and I have done likewise. To do this is every man's business. Everyone has freedom to choose life or reject it. To choose life is to fulfil the will of the Father by doing good to others; to reject it is to do one's own will and not do good to others. It is in each one's power to do the one or the other: to receive life or destroy it.

The true life of man can be compared to this: A master apportioned to his slaves a valuable property and told them each to work on what was given him. Some of them worked, others simply put away what had been given them. Then the master demanded an account of what they had done, and to those who had worked he gave still more of his property, while from those who had not worked he took away all that they had.

The portion of the master's valuable property is the spirit of life in man, who is the son of the Father spirit. He who in this life works for the sake of the spirit-life receives infinite life, he who does not work loses what was given him.

The only true life is the life common to all, and not the life of the individual. Each should work for the life of others.

After that Jesus went to a desert place and many people followed him. Towards evening his pupils came and said: How can we feed all these people?

Among the gathering were some who had no food, and some who had bread and fish. Jesus said to his pupils: Give me what bread you have. And he took the loaves and gave the bread to his pupils, and they gave it away to others, who began to do the same. So everyone ate what was distributed in this way, and they all had enough without eating all the food that was there. And Jesus said: That is how you should always act. It is not necessary for each man to obtain food for himself but it is needful to do what the spirit in man demands, namely to share what there is with others.

The true food of man is the spirit of the Father. Man lives only by the spirit.

We must serve all that has life, for life lies not in doing one's own will but the will of the Father of life. And that will is that the life of the spirit, which each one has, should remain in him and that all should cherish the life of the spirit in them until the hour of death. The Father, the source of all life, is the spirit. Life consists only in carrying out the will of the Father, and to carry out that will of the spirit one must surrender the body. The body is food for the life of the spirit. Only by sacrificing the body does the spirit live.

THE GOSPEL ACCORDING TO SAINT X

After this Jesus chose certain pupils and sent them about to preach the doctrine of the life of the spirit. When sending them he said: You are going to preach the life of the spirit, therefore renounce in advance all fleshly desires and have nothing of your own. Be prepared for persecution, privation, and suffering. Those who love the life of the body will hate you, torment you, and kill you; but do not be afraid. If you fulfil the will of the Father you possess the life of the spirit, of which no one can deprive you.

The pupils set out and when they returned they announced that they had everywhere overcome the teaching of evil.

Then the Orthodox said to Jesus that his teaching, even if it overcame evil, was itself an evil, for those who carry it out must endure sufferings. To this Jesus said: Evil cannot overcome evil. Evil can only be mastered by goodness, and that goodness is the will of the Fatherspirit, common to all men. Every man knows what is good for himself, and if he does that for others-if he does that which is the will of the Father-he will do good. And so the carrying out of the will of the Father-spirit is good even if it be accompanied by the suffering and death of those who fulfil that will.

JESUS said that his mother and his brothers had no prior claim on him as such, only those were never to him who fulfilled the will of their common Father.

A man's life and blessedness depend not on family relationships, but on the life of the spirit. Jesus said: Blessed are those who retain their understanding of the Father. A man living in the spirit has no home-the spirit cannot own a house. He said that he himself had no fixed abode. To fulfil the Father's will no special place is needed, for it is always and everywhere possible.

The death of the body cannot be dreadful to a man who resigns himself to the will of the Father, for the life of the spirit does not depend on that of the body. Jesus says that he who believes in the life of the spirit can fear nothing.

No cares make it impossible for a man to live in the spirit. To one who said that he would obey the teaching of Jesus later, but must first bury his father, Jesus replied: Only the dead trouble about the burial of the dead, the living live always by fulfilling the will of the Father.

Family and household cares must not hinder the life of the spirit. He who is troubled about what results to his bodily life from the fulfilment of the Father's will, acts like a ploughman who looks back while ploughing, instead of in front of him.

Cares for the pleasure of the bodily life, which seem so important to men, are delusions. The only real business of life is the announcement of the Father's will, attention to it, and fulfilment of it. When Martha complained that she alone busied herself about the supper, while her sister Mary listened to his teaching instead of helping, Jesus replied: You blame her unjustly. If you need the results of your work, busy yourself with it, but let those who do not need physical pleasures attend to the one thing essential for life.

Jesus said: He who desires to obtain true life, consisting in the fulfilment of the Father's will, must first of all give up his own personal desires. He must not only not plan his life according to his own wishes, but must be ready to endure privation and suffering at any moment.

He who desires to arrange his bodily life according to his own desires, will wreck the true life of fulfilment of the Father's will. And there is no advantage in gain for the physical life if that gain wrecks the life of the spirit.

Most ruinous of all for the ills of the spirit is the love of gain, of getting rich. Men forget that whatever riches or goods they obtain they may die at any moment, and that property is not essential for life. Death hangs over each of us. Sickness, murder, or accident may at any moment end our life. Bodily death is an inescapable condition of every second of our life. While a man lives he should regard every hour of life as a postponement of death granted by someone's kindness. We should remember this, and not say we do not know it. We know and foresee all that happens on earth and in the sky, but forget death, which we know awaits us at any moment. Unless we forget death we cannot yield ourselves to the life of the body; for we cannot reckon on it. To follow the teaching of Christ we must count up the advantages of following our own will and serving the bodily life, and the advantages of fulfilling the Father's will. Only he who has clearly taken account of this can be a disciple of Christ. But he who makes the calculation will not regret having to forgo this unreal happiness and unreal life in order to obtain the true good and the true life. True life is given to men and they know it and hear its call, but constantly distracted by the cares of the moment they deprive themselves of it. True life is like a feast a rich man gave, and to which he invited guests. He called them-just as the voice of the Father-spirit calls all men to Himself. But some of those invited were busy with trading, others with their farms, others again with family affairs, and they did not go to the feast. Only the poor who had no worldly cares went to the feast and gained happiness. So men distracted by cares for the bodily life deprive themselves of true life. He who does not wholly reject the cares and gains of the bodily life cannot fulfil the Father's will, for no man can serve himself a little and the Father a little: he has to consider whether it is better to serve his body and whether it is possible to arrange his life according to his own will. He must do as a man does who wishes to build a house, or to prepare for war. That man first considers whether he has means to finish his house, or to conquer his enemy. And if he sees that he has not, he will not waste his labor or his army uselessly, and make himself a laughing-stock to his neighbors. If a man could arrange his bodily life to his own will, then it might be well to serve the body, but as that is impossible, it is better to reject bodily things and serve the spirit. Otherwise you will gain neither the one thing nor the other. You will not arrange the bodily life satisfactorily, and will lose the life of the spirit. Therefore to fulfil the Father's will it is necessary to sacrifice the bodily life.

The bodily life is wealth entrusted to us by another, which we should use so as to gain our own true riches.

If a rich man has a manager who knows that however well he may serve his master, that master will dismiss him leaving him with nothing, the manager will be wise if while managing his master's affairs he does favors to other people. Then when the master dismisses him, those whom he has benefited will receive him and sustain him. That is how men deal in their bodily life. The bodily life is that wealth, not our own, which is entrusted to us for a time. If we make good use of that wealth which is not our own, then we shall receive true wealth which will be our own.

If we do not give up wealth that is not our own, we shall not receive our true wealth. We cannot serve both the illusory life of the body and the life of the spirit; we must serve the one or the other. A man cannot serve property and God. What is honorable among men is an abomination before God. In God's sight riches are evil. A rich man is guilty in that he eats much and luxuriously, while at his door the poor are hungry. And everyone knows that property not shared with others is held in non-fulfilment of the Father's will.

A rich, Orthodox ruler came once to Jesus and began to boast that he fulfilled all the commandments of the law. Jesus reminded him that there is a commandment to love others as oneself and that that is the Father's will. The ruler said he kept that also. Then Jesus said to him: That is not true; if you really wished to fulfil the Father's will you would not possess property. You cannot fulfil the Father's will if you have property of your own which you do not give to others. And Jesus said to his pupils: Men think it impossible to live without property, but I tell you that true life consists in giving what you have to others.

A certain man named Zaccheus heard the teaching of Jesus and believed it, and having invited Jesus to his house said to him: I am giving half my fortune to the poor and will restore fourfold to those I have wronged. And Jesus said: Here is a man who fulfills the Father's will, for a man's whole life must be passed in fulfilment of that will, and there is no condition in which a man can say: 'I have fulfilled the will of God.'

Good cannot be measured; it is impossible to say who has done more or less. A widow who gives away her last farthing gives more than a rich man who gives thousands. Nor can goodness be measured by its usefulness.

Let the case of the woman who felt pity for Jesus and recklessly poured over his feet many pounds' worth of costly oil serve as an example. Judas said she had acted foolishly because the cost of the oil would have sufficed to feed many people. But Judas was a thief and a liar, and when he spoke of the material advantage he was not thinking of the poor. The essential thing lies not in the utility of an action or the largeness of a gift, but what is necessary is always, every moment, to love others and give them what one has.

ANSWERING the Jews' demand for proofs of the truth of his teaching, Jesus said: The truth of my teaching lies in the fact that I teach not something of my own but what comes from the common Father of us all. I teach what is good for the Father of all and is therefore good for all men.

BOB PROPHETTE

Do what I say, fulfil the five commandments, and you will see that what I say is true. Fulfillment of these five commandments will drive away all evil from the world, and therefore they are certainly true. It is clear that he who teaches the will of Him who sent him, and not his own will, teaches the truth. The law of Moses teaches the fulfilment of human desires and so it is full of contradictions; my teaching is to fulfil the will of the Father and so it is harmonious.

The Jews did not understand him and looked for external proofs of whether he was the Christ mentioned in the prophecies. On this he said to them: Do not question who I am and whether it is of me that your prophecies speak, but attend to my teaching and to what I say about our common Father.

You need not believe in me as a man, but you should believe what I tell you in the name of the common Father of us all.

It is not necessary to inquire about external matters as to where I come from, but it is necessary to follow my teaching. He who follows it will receive true life. There can be no proofs of the truth of my teaching. It is the light itself, and as light cannot be illuminated, so truth cannot be proven true. My teaching is the light. He who sees it has light and life and needs no proofs, but he who is in darkness must come to the light.

But the Jews again asked him who he was as to his bodily personality. He said to them: I am, as I told you from the first, a man, the son of the Father of life. Only he who so regards himself (this is the truth I teach) will fulfil the will of the common Father; only he will cease to be a slave and become a free man. We are enslaved only by the error of taking the life of the body to be the true life. He who understands the truth-that life consists only in the fulfilment of the Father's will—becomes free and immortal. As a slave does not always remain in the house of his master, but the son does; so a man who lives as a slave to the flesh does not remain alive for ever, but he who fulfills in his soul the Father's will has eternal life. To understand me you must understand that my Father is not the same as your father whom you call God. Your father is a god of the flesh, but my Father is the spirit of life. Your father, your god, is a jealous god, a man-slayer, one who executes men. My Father gives life, and so we are the children of different fathers. I seek the truth, and you wish to kill me for that, to please your god. Your god is the devil, the source of evil, and in serving him you serve the devil. My teaching is that we are sons of the Father of life, and he who believes in my teaching shall not see death. The Jews asked: How can it be that a man will not die, when all those who pleased God most—even Abraham—have died? How then can you say that you, and those who believe in your teaching, will not die?

To this Jesus replied: I speak not by my own authority. I speak of that same source of life that you call God, and that dwells in men. That source I know and cannot help knowing, and I know His will and fulfil it, and of that source of life I say that it has been, is, and will be, and that for it there is no death.

Demands for proofs of the truth of my teaching are as if one demanded from a man who had been born blind, proofs of why and how he sees the light when his sight has been restored.

The blind man whose sight has been restored, remaining the same man he was, can only say that he was blind but now sees. And one who formerly did not understand the meaning of life but now does understand it, can only say the same, and nothing else.

Such a man can only say that formerly he did not know the true good in life but now he knows it. A blind man whose sight has been restored, if told that he has not been cured in a proper manner and that he, who restored his sight is an evil-doer, and that he should be cured differently, can only reply: I know nothing about the correctness of my cure or the sinfulness of him who cured me, or of a better way of being cured; I only know that whereas I was blind, now I see. And in the same way one who has understood the meaning of the teaching of true welfare and of the fulfilment of the Father's will, can say nothing as to the regularity of that teaching or whether he who disclosed it to him was a sinner, or of the possibility of a still greater blessedness, but can only say: Formerly I did not see the meaning of life, but now I see it and that is all I know.

And Jesus said: My teaching is the awakening of a life till then asleep: he who believes my teaching awakens to eternal life and lives after death.

My teaching is not proven in any way: men yield to it because it alone has the promise of life for all men.

As sheep follow the shepherd who gives them food and guards their life, so men accept my teaching because it gives life to all. And as the sheep do not follow a thief who climbs over into the fold, but shy away from him, so men cannot believe these doctrines which teach violence and executions. My teaching is as a door for the sheep, and all who follow me shall find true life. As only those shepherds are good who own and love the sheep and devote their lives to them, while hirelings who do not love the sheep are bad shepherds, so also only that teacher is true who does not spare himself, and he is worthless who cares only for himself. My teaching is that a man should not spare himself, but should sacrifice the life of the body for the life of the spirit. This I teach and fulfil.

THE GOSPEL ACCORDING TO SAINT X

The Jews still did not understand and still wanted proofs of whether or not Jesus was the Christ, and whether, therefore, they should believe him or not. They said: Do not torment us, but tell us plainly, are you the Christ or not? And to this Jesus replied: Belief must be given not to words but to deeds. By the example I set, you may know whether I teach the truth or not. Do what I do, and do not discuss words. Fulfil the will of the Father, and then you will all be united with me and with the Father; for I, the son of man, am the same as the Father and the same that you call God and that I call the Father. I and the Father are one. Even in your own scriptures it is said that God said to men: 'You are Gods.' Every man by his spirit is a son of this Father. And if a man lives fulfilling the Father's will he becomes one with the Father. If I fulfil His will, the Father is in me and I am in the Father.

After this Jesus asked his pupils how they understood his teaching about the son of man. Simon Peter answered him: Your teaching is that you are the son of the God of life, and God is the life of the spirit in man. And Jesus said to him: You are happy, Simon, to have understood that. Man could not have disclosed it to you, but you have understood it because the God in you has revealed it to you. On this understanding the true life of men is founded. For that life there is no death.

In reply to doubts expressed by his pupils as to the reward resulting for renouncing the life of the flesh, Jesus said: For him who understands the meaning of my teaching there can be no question of a reward, first because a man who for its sake gives up family, friends, and possessions, gains a hundredfold more friends and more possessions, and secondly, because a man who seeks a reward seeks to have more than others have, and that is quite contrary to the fulfilment of the Father's will. In the kingdom of heaven there is neither greater nor less, all are equal. Those who seek a reward for goodness are like laborers who, because in their opinion they were more deserving than others, demanded larger pay than they had agreed upon with their employer. According to the teaching of Jesus no one can be either higher or more important than another.

All can fulfil the Father's will, but in doing so no one becomes superior or more important or better than another. Only kings and those who serve them reckon in that way. According to my teaching, said Jesus, there can be no superior rank; he who wishes to be better should be the servant of all. My teaching is, that life is given to man not that others may serve him, but that he should give his whole life to the service of others. He who exalts himself instead of doing this, will fall lower than he was.

The meaning and purpose of life must be understood before a man can be rid of thoughts of his own elevation. The meaning of life lies in fulfilling the will of the Father, and His will is that what He has given us shall be returned to Him. As a shepherd leaves his whole flock and goes to seek a lost sheep, and as a woman will search everywhere to find a lost penny, so the Father's continual work is manifested to us by the fact that He draws to Himself that which pertains to Him.

We must understand wherein true life consists. True life always appears in the lost being restored to where it belongs, and in the awakening of those that sleep. People who have the true life and have returned to the source of their being, cannot, like worldly men, account others as being better or worse, but being sharers of the Father's life can only rejoice at the return of the lost to the Father. If a son who has gone astray repents and returns to the father he had left, how can other sons of the same father be envious of his joy, or fail to rejoice at their brother's return?

THE GOSPEL ACCORDING TO SAINT X

To believe in the teaching and to change our way of life and fulfil that teaching, what is needed is not external proofs or promises of rewards, but a clear understanding of what true life is. If men think themselves completely masters of their own lives, and believe that life is given them for bodily enjoyment, then clearly any sacrifice they make for others will seem to them an act worthy of reward, and without such reward they will give nothing. If tenants forgot that a garden was let to them on condition that they returned the fruits to the owner, and that rent was demanded of them again and again, they would seek to kill the collector. So it is with those who think themselves masters of their own lives and do not understand that life is granted them by an understanding which demands the fulfilment of its will. To believe and to act, it is necessary to understand that man can do nothing of himself, and that if he gives up his bodily life to serve goodness he does nothing that deserves either thanks or reward. We must understand that in doing good a man only does his duty and what he necessarily must do. Only when he understands life in that way can a man have faith enabling him to do truly good deeds.

The kingdom of heaven consists in that understanding of life. It is not a visible kingdom that can be pointed out in this or that place. The kingdom of heaven is in man's understanding. The whole world lives as of old: men eat and drink, marry, trade, and die, and along with this in the souls of men lives the kingdom of heaven-an understanding of life growing as a tree that in spring puts out leaves of itself.

True life is the fulfilment of the will of the Father, not in the past or in the future, but now; it is what each of us must do at the present moment. And therefore to live the true life we must never relax. Men are set to guard life, not in the past or in the future, but the life now being lived, and in it to fulfil the will of the Father of all men. If they let this life escape them by not fulfilling the Father's will, they will not receive it back again. A watchman set to watch all night does not perform his duty if he falls asleep even for a moment, for a thief may come at that moment. So man should direct his whole strength to the present hour, for only then can he fulfil the Father's will; and that will is the life and blessing of all men. Only those live who are doing good. Good done to men now in the present, is the life that unites us with the common Father.

MAN is born with a knowledge of the true life which lies in the fulfilment of the Father's will. Children live by that knowledge: in them the will of the Father is seen. To understand the teaching of Jesus one must understand the life of children and be like them.

Children live in the Father's will, not infringing the five commandments, and they would never infringe them were they not misled by adults. Men ruin children by leading them to break these commandments. And by so doing they act as if they tied a millstone to a man's neck and threw him into the river. The world is unhappy only because people yield to temptations, but for that the world would be happy. Temptations lure men to do evil for the sake of imaginary advantages in their temporal life. Yielding to temptation ruins men, and therefore everything should be sacrificed rather than fall into temptation.

The temptation to infringe the first commandment comes from men considering themselves in the right towards others, and others in the wrong towards themselves. To avoid falling into that temptation we must remember that all men are always infinitely in debt to the Father and can only acquit themselves of that debt by forgiving their brother men.

Therefore men must forgive injuries, and not be deterred though the offender injures them again and again. However often a man may be wronged he must forgive, not remembering the wrong; for only by forgiveness can the kingdom of heaven be attained. If we do not forgive others, we act as a certain debtor did when, heavily in debt, he went to his creditor and begged for mercy. His creditor forgave him everything, but the debtor went away and meeting a man who owed him only a small sum, began to throttle him. To have life we must fulfil the Father's will. We ask forgiveness of Him for failing to fulfil His will, and hope to be forgiven. What then are we doing if we do not ourselves forgive others? We are doing to them what we dread for ourselves.

The will of the Father is well-being; and evil is that which separates us from the Father. How then can we fail to seek to quench evil as quickly as possible, since it is that which ruins us and robs us of life? Evil entangles us in bodily destruction. In so far as we escape from that entanglement we obtain life and have all that we can desire. We are not separated from one another by evil but are united by love.

Men are tempted to infringe the second commandment by thinking of woman as created for bodily pleasure, and by supposing that by leaving one wife and taking another they will obtain more pleasure. To avoid falling into this temptation we must remember that the Father's will is, not that man should delight himself with woman's charms, but that each man having chosen a wife should be one with her. The Father's will is for each man to have one wife and each wife one husband. If each man keeps to one wife, each man will have a wife and each woman a husband. He who changes his wife deprives her of a husband and gives occasion for some other man to leave his wife and take the deserted one. A man need not marry at all, but must not have more than one wife, for if he does he goes against the will of the Father which is that one man should unite with one woman.

BOB PROPHETTE

Men are tempted to infringe the third commandment by creating, for the advantage of their temporal life, established authorities, and demanding from one another oaths by which they bind themselves to do what those authorities demand. To avoid falling into this temptation men must remember that they are indebted for their life to no power but God. The demands of authorities should be regarded as violence but, following the command of non-resistance to evil, men should yield what goods and labor the authorities may demand. But they must not pledge their conduct by taking oaths, for the oaths that are imposed lead to evil. He who recognizes his life as being in the will of the Father cannot bind his actions by pledges, for such a man holds his life most sacred.

Men are tempted to infringe the fourth commandment by thinking that they can reform others by themselves yielding to anger and revenge. If a man wrongs another, people think he should be punished and that justice lies in human judgment.

To avoid falling into this temptation we must remember that men are called not to judge but to save one another, and that they cannot judge one another's faults because they are themselves full of wickedness. The one thing they can do is to teach others by an example of purity, forgiveness, and love.

Men are tempted to infringe the fifth commandment by thinking that there is a difference between their own countrymen and those of other nations, and that it is therefore necessary to defend themselves against other nations and do them harm. To avoid falling into this temptation it is necessary to know that all the commandments may be summed up in this: to do good to all men without distinction, and thus fulfil the will of the Father who has given life and well-being to all. Even if others make such distinctions, and though nations, considering themselves alien to one another, go to war, yet each man, to fulfil the will of the Father, should do good to all-even to those belonging to a nation with which his country is at war.

To avoid falling into human illusions we must think not of the physical but the spiritual life. If a man understands that life consists solely in now being in the Father's will, neither privations, nor sufferings, nor death, can seem dreadful to him. Only that man receives true life who is ready at every moment to give up his physical life in order to fulfil the Father's will.

And that everyone may understand that true life is that in which there is no death, Jesus said: Eternal life should not be understood as being like the present life. For true life in the will of the Father there is neither space nor time.

Those who are awake to the true life live in the Father's will for which there is neither space nor time. They live with the Father. If they have died for us, they live for God. Therefore one commandment includes in itself all: to love all men, each of whom has the source of life within him.

And Jesus said: That source of life is the Christ you are awaiting. The comprehension of that source of life, for whom there is no distinction of persons and no time or place, is the son of man whom I teach. All that hides that source of life, from men is temptation. There is the temptation of the scribes, of the bookmen, and of the materialists- do not yield to it. There is the temptation of authority, do not yield to that: and there is also the most terrible temptation, from the religious teachers who call themselves Orthodox. Beware of this last temptation more than of all the others, because these self-ordained teachers, just they, by devising the worship of a false God decoy you from the true God. Instead of serving the Father of life by deeds, they substitute words, and teach words while they themselves do nothing.

BOB PROPHETTE

You can learn nothing from them but words, and the Father requires deed. They can teach nothing because they themselves know nothing, and only for their own advantage A wish to set themselves up as teachers. But you know that no man can be the teacher of another. There is one teacher for all men-the Lord of life the understanding. But these self-styled teachers, thinking to teach others, deprive themselves of true life and hinder others from understanding it. They teach men that their God will be pleased by external rites, and think they can bring men to religion by vows. They are only concerned about externals. An outward assumption of religion satisfies them, but they do not think of what goes on in men's hearts. And so they are like showy sepulchres, handsome outside but loathsome within. In words they honor the saints and the martyrs, but they are just the people who formerly killed and tortured and who now kill and torture the saints. From them come all the world's temptations for under the guise of good they teach evil.

The evil they create is the root of all others, for they defile the most holy thing in the world. They will continue their deceptions and increase evil in the world, and it will be long before they are changed. But a time will come when all their churches and all external worship of God will be destroyed, and men will understand, and unite in love, to serve the one God of life and to fulfil His will.

THE Jews saw that the teaching of Jesus would destroy their State religion and their nationality, and at the same time saw that they could not refute it, so they decided to kill him. His innocence and rectitude hindered them but the high priest Caiaphas devised a pretext for killing him even though Jesus was not guilty in any way. Caiaphas said: We need not discuss whether this man is innocent or guilty; we have to consider whether we wish our people to remain a separate Jewish nation or whether we wish it to be broken

THE GOSPEL ACCORDING TO SAINT X

up and dispersed. The nation will perish and the people be scattered if we let this man alone and do not put him to death. This argument decided the matter, and the Orthodox agreed that Jesus must be put to death; and they instructed the people to seize him as soon as he appeared in Jerusalem.

Though he knew of this, Jesus nevertheless went to Jerusalem for the feast of the Passover. His pupils entreated him not to go, but he said: What the Orthodox wish to do to me, and all that any man may do, cannot alter the truth for me. If I see the light I know where I am and where I am going. Only he who does not know the truth can fear anything or doubt anything. Only he who does not see, stumbles. And he went to Jerusalem, stopping on the way at Bethany. There Mary emptied a jar of precious oil on him, and when the pupils reproached her for wasting so much precious oil, Jesus, knowing that his bodily death was near at hand, said that what she had done was a preparation for his burial. When he left Bethany and went to Jerusalem crowds met and followed him, and this convinced the Orthodox still more of the need to kill him. They only wanted an opportunity to seize him. He knew that the least indiscreet word from him now, contrary to the law, would be used as a reason for his execution; but notwithstanding this he went into the temple and again declared that the Jewish worship of God with sacrifices and libations was false, and he again announced his teaching. But his teaching, based on the prophets, was such that the Orthodox could still find no palpable breach of this law for which they could condemn him to death, especially as most of the common people were on his side. But at the feast there were certain heathen who having heard of Jesus's teaching, wished to discuss it with him. The pupils hearing of this were alarmed. They feared lest Jesus by talking with the heathen might betray himself and excite the people. At first they did not want to put the heathen in touch with Jesus, but afterwards they decided to tell him that these men wished to speak with him. On hearing this, Jesus was troubled. He understood that his talk with the heathen would make clear his rejection of the whole Jewish law, would turn the crowd from him, and would give occasion to the Orthodox to accuse him of having intercourse with the hated heathen; and knowing this he was troubled. But he also knew that his mission was to make clear to men, the sons of one Father, their unity without distinction of faith. He knew that to do this would cost him his bodily life but that its loss would give men a true understanding of life, and therefore he said: As a grain of wheat perishes to bear fruit, so I, a man, must give up my bodily life in order to bear spiritual fruit. He who holds fast to his bodily life loses his true life, but he who does not grudge his bodily life obtains the true life. I am troubled at what awaits me, but I have lived till now only in preparation for this hour, how then can I fail to act as I ought? So let the Father's will be manifested through me now.

And turning to the people, heathen and Jews, Jesus declared openly what he had only said privately to Nicodemus. He said: Men's lives, with their different creeds and governments, must all be changed. All human authorities must disappear. It is only necessary to understand the nature of man as a son of the Father of life, and this understanding destroys all divisions of men and of authorities and makes all men one. The Jews said: You are destroying our whole creed. Our law tells of a Christ, but you speak only of a Son of Man and say that he should be exalted What does that mean? He replied: To exalt the son of man means living by the light of understanding that exists in man, and while there is light, living by that light. I teach no new faith but only what each man may know within himself. Each man knows the life in himself, and each man knows that life is given to him and to all men by the Father of life. My teaching is only that man should love the life that the Father gives to us all.

Many of the unofficial folk believed Jesus; but the notables and official classes did not believe him, because they did not wish to consider the universal purport of what he said, and thought only of its temporal bearings. They saw that he turned the people from them and they wished to kill him; but they feared to take him openly, and wanted to do so secretly not in Jerusalem and in the daytime. And one of his twelve pupils, Judas Iscariot, came to them, and they bribed him to take their emissaries to Jesus when he should be away from the people. Judas promised to do this, and went back to Jesus, awaiting a suitable opportunity to betray him. On the first day of the feast Jesus kept the Passover with his pupils, and Judas, thinking that Jesus was not aware of his treachery, was with them. But Jesus knew that Judas had sold him, and as they all sat at table he took bread, broke it into twelve pieces, and gave one to each of the pupils, to Judas as well as to the others, and without naming anyone, said: Take, eat my body. Then he took a cup with wine, gave it to them all, including Judas, to drink, and said: One of you will shed my blood. Drink my blood. Then he rose and washed all the pupils' feet, and when he had done so said: I know that one of you will betray me to death and will shed my blood, but I have fed him and given him drink and washed his feet. I have done this to show you how to behave to those who harm you. If you act so, you will be blessed. And the pupils all asked which of them was the betrayer. But Jesus did not name him, that they might not turn on him. When it grew dark, however, Jesus indicated Judas and at the same time told him to go away, and Judas got up from the table and went off and no one hindered him. Then Jesus said: This is what it means to exalt the son of man. To exalt the son of man is to be as kind as the Father not only to those who love us but to all men, even to those who do us harm. Therefore do not argue about my teaching, do not pick it to pieces as the Orthodox do, but do as I do and as I have now done before your eyes. This one commandment I give you: love men. My whole teaching is to love men always and to the end . After this, fear came over Jesus, and he went in the dark with his pupils to a garden to be out of the way. And on the road he said to them: You are all of you wavering and timid; if they come to take me you will all run away. To this Peter replied: No, I will never desert you and will defend you even to the death. And the other pupils all said the same.

Then Jesus said: If that is so, then prepare for defence, get weapons to defend yourselves and collect your provisions, for we shall have to hide. The pupils replied that they had two knives. When Jesus heard the mention of knives, anguish came over him. And going to a lonely spot he began to pray and urged the pupils to do the same, but they did not understand him. Jesus said: My Father-the spirit! End in me this struggle with temptation. Confirm me in the fulfilment of Thy will. I want to overcome my own wish to defend my bodily life, and to do Thy will-not resisting evil. The pupils still did not understand. And he said to them: Do not consider the body, but try to exalt the spirit in yourselves; strength is in the spirit, but the flesh is weak. And again he said: My Father! If suffering must be, then let it come: but in the suffering I want one thing only, that not my will, but Thine, may be fulfilled in me. The pupils did not understand. And again he strove with temptation and at last overcame it; and coming to his pupils he said: Now it is decided, you can be at rest. I shall not fight, but shall give myself up into the hands of the men of this world.

And Jesus, feeling himself prepared for death, went to give himself up, but Peter stopped him and asked where he was going. Jesus replied: I am going where you cannot go. I am ready for death, but you are not yet ready for it. Peter said: I am ready to give my life for you now. Jesus replied: A man cannot pledge himself to anything. And he said to all his pupils: I know that death awaits me, but I believe in the life of the Father and therefore do not fear it. Do not be disturbed at my death, but believe in the true God and Father of life, and then my death will not seem dreadful to you. If I am United to the Father of life, then I cannot be deprived of life. It is true that I do not tell you what or where my life after death will be, but I point out to you the way to true life. My teaching does not tell you what that life is to be, but it reveals the only true path to that life, which is to be in unity with the Father. The Father is the source of life. My teaching is that man should live in the will of the Father and fulfil His will for the life and welfare of all men. Your teacher when I am gone will be your knowledge of the truth. In fulfilling my teaching on will always feel that you are in the truth and you in the Father. That the Father is in you. And knowing the Father of life in yourselves, you will experience a peace nothing can deprive you of. And therefore if you know the truth and live in it, neither my death nor your own can alarm you.

Men think of themselves as separate beings, each with his own separate will to live, but that is only an illusion. The only true life is that which recognizes the Father's will as the source of life. My teaching reveals this oneness of life, and presents life not as separate growths but as one tree on which all the branches grow. Only he lives who lives in the Father's will like a branch on its parent tree: he who wishes to live by his own will dies like a branch that has been torn away. The Father gave me life to do good, and I have taught you to live to do good. If you fulfil my commandments you will be blessed, and the commandment which sums up my whole teaching is simply that all men should love one another. And love is to sacrifice the bodily life for the sake of another: there is no other definition.

And in fulfilling my law of love you will not fulfil it like slaves who obey their master's orders without understanding them; but you will live as free men like myself, for I have made clear to you the purpose of life flowing from a knowledge of the Father of life. You have received my teaching not because you accidentally chose it, but because it is the only truth by which men are made free.

The teaching of the world is that men should do evil to one another, but my teaching is that they should love one another. Therefore the world will hate you as it has hated me. The world does not understand my teaching and therefore will persecute you and do you harm, thinking to serve God by so doing. Do not be surprised at this, but understand that it must be so. The world, not understanding the true God, must persecute you, but you must affirm the truth.

You are distressed at their killing me, but they kill me for declaring the truth, and my death is necessary for the confirmation of the truth. My death, at which I do not recede from the truth will strengthen you, and you will understand what is false and what is true and what results from a knowledge of falsehood and of truth. You will understand that it is falsehood for men to believe in the bodily life and not in the life of the spirit, and that truth consists in unity with the Father from which results the victory of the spirit over the flesh.

When I am no longer with you in the bodily life, my spirit will be with you; but like all men you will not always feel within you the strength of the spirit. Sometimes you will weaken and lose the strength of the spirit and fall into temptation, and sometimes you will again awaken to the true life.

Hours of bondage to the flesh will come upon you, but only for a time; you will suffer and be again restored to the spirit as a woman suffers in childbirth and then feels joy that she has brought a human being into the world. You will experience the same when after being enslaved by the body you again rise in spirit, and feel such joy that there will be nothing more for you to desire. Know this in advance: in despite of persecution, of inward struggle and depression of spirit, the spirit lives within you and the one true God is the knowledge of the Father's will that I have revealed.

And addressing the Father, the spirit, Jesus said: I have done what Thou commanded me, and have revealed to men that Thou art the source of all things, and they have understood me. I have taught them that they all come from one source of infinite life and that therefore they are all one, and that as the Father is in me and I am in the Father, so they, too, are one with me and the Father. I have revealed to them also that as Thou in love hast sent them into the world, they too should serve the world by love.

When Jesus had finished speaking to his pupils, he rose and, instead of running away or defending himself, went to meet Judas who was bringing soldiers to take him. Jesus went to him and asked him why he had come. But Judas did not answer and a crowd of soldiers came round Jesus. Peter rushed to defend him and, drawing a knife, began to fight. But Jesus stopped him and told him to give up the knife, saying that he who fights with a knife himself perishes by a knife. Then he said to those who had come to take him: I have till now gone about among you alone without fear, and I feel no fear now, I give myself up to you to do with me as you please. And all his pupils ran away and deserted him. Then the officer of the soldiers ordered Jesus to be bound and taken to Annas, a former high priest who lived in the same house as Caiaphas, who was high priest that year and who had devised the pretext upon which it was decided to kill Jesus: namely, that if he were not killed the whole nation would perish. Jesus, feeling himself in the will of the Father, was ready for death and did not resist when they took him, and was not afraid when they led him away; but that very Peter who had just assured Jesus that he would rather die than renounce him, the same Peter who had tried to defend Jesus, now when he saw Jesus being led to execution was afraid they would execute him too, and when the doorkeeper asked whether he had not been with Jesus, denied him and deserted him. Only later, when the cock crowed, did Peter understand all that Jesus had said to him. He understood that there are two temptations of the flesh-fear and strife-and that Jesus had resisted these when he prayed in the garden and asked the pupils to pray. And now he, Peter, had yielded to both these temptations against which Jesus had warned him: he had tried to resist evil and to defend the truth had been ready to fight and do evil himself; and now in fear of bodily suffering he had renounced his master. Jesus had not yielded either to the temptation to fight when the pupils had two knives ready for his defence, or to the temptation of fear-first before the people in Jerusalem when the heathen wished to speak to him, and now before the soldiers when they bound him and led him to trial.

Jesus was brought before Caiaphas, who began to question him about his teaching. But knowing that Caiaphas asked not to find out about his teaching but only to convict him, Jesus did not reply, but said: I have concealed nothing and conceal nothing now: if you wish to know what my teaching is, ask those who heard it and understood it. For this answer the high priest's servant struck Jesus on the cheek. Jesus asked why he struck him, but the man did not answer him and the high priest continued the trial. Witnesses were brought and gave evidence that Jesus had boasted that he would destroy the Jewish faith. And the high priest questioned Jesus, but seeing that they did not ask in order to learn anything, but only to pretend that it was a just trial, he answered nothing.

Then the high priest asked him: Tell me, are you Christ, a son of God? Jesus said: Yes, I am Christ, a son of God; and now in torturing me you will see how the son of man resembles God.

The high priest was glad to hear these words and said to the other judges: Are not these words enough to condemn him? And the judges said: They are enough: we sentence him to death. And when they said this, the people threw themselves upon Jesus and began to strike him, to spit in his face, and to insult him. He remained silent.

The Jews had not the right to put anyone to death: to do this permission was needed from the Roman governor. So having condemned, Jesus in their court, and having subjected him to ignominy, they took him to the Roman governor Pilate that he might order his execution. Pilate asked why they wished to put Jesus to death, and they answered that he was a criminal. Pilate said that if that was so, they should judge him by their own law. They answered: We want you to put him to death, because he is guilty before the Roman Caesar: he is a rebel, he agitates the people, forbids them to pay taxes to Caesar, and calls himself the King of the Jews. Pilate called Jesus before him, and said: What is the meaning of this, are you King of the Jews? Jesus said: Do you really wish to know what my kingdom is, or are you only asking me for form's sake? Pilate answered: I am not a Jew, and it is the same to me whether you call yourself King of the Jews or not, but I ask you who you are and why do they call you a king? Jesus replied: They say truly that I call myself a king. I am indeed a king, but my kingdom is not an earthly one, it is a heavenly one. Earthly kings have armies and go to war and fight, but as you see they have bound and beaten me and I did not resist. I am a heavenly king and my power is in the spirit.

Pilate said: So it is true that you consider yourself a king? Jesus replied: You know it yourself. Everyone who lives by the spirit is free. I live by this alone, and teach only to show men the truth that they are free if they live by the spirit. Pilate said: You teach the truth, but nobody knows what truth is. Everyone has his own truth. And having said this he turned away from Jesus and went back again to the Jews, and said: I find nothing criminal in this man. Why do you wish me to put him to death? The chief priests said: He ought to be executed because he stirs up the people. Then Pilate began to examine Jesus before the chief priests, but Jesus, seeing that this was only for form's sake, answered nothing. Then Pilate said: I alone cannot condemn him. Take him to Herod.

At the trial before Herod, Jesus again did not answer the chief priests' accusations, and Herod, taking Jesus to be an empty fellow, mockingly ordered him to be dressed in a red cloak and sent back to Pilate. Pilate pitied Jesus and began to persuade the chief priests to forgive him, if only on account of the feast; but they held to their demand, and they all, and the people with them, cried out to have Jesus crucified. Pilate again tried to persuade them to let Jesus go, but the priests and the people cried out that he must be executed. They said: He is guilty of calling himself a son of God. Pilate again called Jesus to him, and asked. What does it mean that you call yourself a son of God? Who are you? Jesus answered nothing. Then Pilate said: How is it that you do not answer me, when I have the power to execute you or to set you free? Jesus replied: You have no power over me. All power is from above. And Pilate for the third time tried to persuade the Jews to set Jesus free, but they said to him: If you will not execute this man whom we have denounced as a rebel against Caesar, then you yourself are not a friend to Caesar, but a foe. And on hearing these words Pilate gave way and ordered the execution of Jesus. But they first stripped Jesus and flogged him, and then dressed him again in the red cloak. And they beat him and insulted him and mocked him. Then they gave him a cross to carry and led him to the place of execution, and there they nailed him to the cross, and as he hung on the cross the people all mocked at him. And to this mockery Jesus answered: Father, do not punish them for this, they do not know what they are doing. And later, when he was already near to death, he said: My Father! Into Thy care I yield my spirit. And bowing his head he breathed his last.

About Bob Prophette

Bob Prophette is a Priest, Bookie and Judge. A Welsh-Irish-Canadian, born in 1967 in Toronto to Irish parents, he lived in Ireland, England and Wales as a child. He is a dad, analyst, researcher, artist, piss taker, strummer, writer, singer, dancer, deep diver, fool, shaman and prophette.

As an author Bob's work is mainly appropriation. Using existing texts in new ways to make a point that would be much more difficult to make otherwise.

Other books by Bob Prophette include:

> The Book of Revelation as Revealed to Bob Prophette. The Bible's most mysterious book given the Dr Seuss treatment with illustrations by Albrecht Dürer.
>
> The Suffering of Pooh: The Bible's Book of Job retold by the cast of the Winnie the Pooh books.
>
> The Female Bible: 1000+ passages from the Bible mentioning women. A roller-coaster ride of ritualized sexism, exploitation and abuse.
>
> The Good Book: An edited version of the King James Bible with all the crap taken out. The Bible exorcised! Fits in your pocket.

Bob can be contacted via Bobprophette.com

www.ingramcontent.com/pod-product-compliance
Lightning Source LLC
Chambersburg PA
CBHW011232160426
43209CB00010B/1562